LOOKING AT HISTORY:
QUEEN ANNE TO QUEEN ELIZABETH II

By means of hundreds of pictures the social history of England through the ages is shown vividly and with a wealth of authentic detail.

In this fourth volume of LOOKING AT HISTORY R. J. Unstead tells how the people lived, worked, travelled and enjoyed themselves from 1714 up to the present day. He also tells you about some of the wonderful inventions and discoveries made in the twentieth century.

'An excellent introduction to the concrete details of the past.'

Times Literary Supplement

3 bcd

Other books by R. J. Unstead

THE STORY OF BRITAIN: BEFORE THE NORMAN CONQUEST
THE STORY OF BRITAIN: IN THE MIDDLE AGES
THE STORY OF BRITAIN: IN TUDOR AND STUART TIMES
THE STORY OF BRITAIN: FROM WILLIAM OF ORANGE TO WORLD WAR II
SOME KINGS AND QUEENS
ROYAL ADVENTURERS
PRINCES AND REBELS
DISCOVERERS AND ADVENTURERS
GREAT LEADERS
HEROES AND SAINTS
PEOPLE IN HISTORY: FROM CARACTACUS TO ALFRED
LOOKING AT HISTORY: FROM CAVEMEN TO VIKINGS
LOOKING AT HISTORY: THE MIDDLE AGES
LOOKING AT HISTORY: TUDORS AND STUARTS

and published by CAROUSEL BOOKS

ABOUT THIS BOOK

This book tells how the people of England lived, worked, travelled and enjoyed themselves from 1714 up to the present day.

Although it does not devote very much space to wars, battles and famous people, the chief events and people of these times are mentioned, and a fuller account can be found in other history books.

It would take a book many times the length of this one to show the many wonderful inventions and discoveries made in the twentieth century. For the most part, I have chosen those which have affected our way of life in this century. We must not forget, however, the great progress that has been made in medicine, science, shipping, building, engineering, mining, farming and industry, and the arrival of new fabrics such as nylon and plastic, new medicines such as M. and B. and penicillin, and new weapons such as the atomic bomb and the long-range rocket.

LOOKING AT HISTORY: QUEEN ANNE
TO QUEEN ELIZABETH II

A CAROUSEL BOOK 0 552 54070 6

Originally published in Great Britain by
A. & C. Black Ltd.

PRINTING HISTORY

A. & C. Black edition published 1953
A. & C. Black edition reprinted many times
A. & C. Black edition reissued 1961
A. & C. Black edition reprinted 1964
A. & C. Black edition reprinted 1966
Carousel edition published 1975

Carousel Books are published by Transworld Publishers Ltd, Cavendish House, 57-59 Uxbridge Road, Ealing, London W5.

Printed by James Paton Ltd., Paisley.

LOOKING AT HISTORY

R. J. UNSTEAD

Book IV
QUEEN ANNE TO
QUEEN ELIZABETH II

Consultant editor: Anne Wood

CAROUSEL BOOKS
A DIVISION OF TRANSWORLD PUBLISHERS LTD

CONTENTS
PART ONE   LIFE IN GEORGIAN ENGLAND

PART ONE LIFE IN GEORGIAN ENGLAND

SOME PEOPLE AND EVENTS

The Kings of England during this period were:

George I (1714–1727) A German relation of Queen Anne, who became King because the Catholic Stuarts were debarred from the throne.

George II (1727–1760)

George III (1760–1820)

George IV (1820–1830)

William IV (1830–1837)

THE JACOBITES. 'The Fifteen' and 'The Forty-Five' Risings.

In 1715, James II's son, *James Edward*, 'The Pretender,' tried to win back his father's throne with Scottish help, but he failed dismally. His son, *Bonnie Prince Charlie*, made a bolder attempt in 1745, and frightened the English government by marching south as far as Derby. Eventually, his Highlanders were utterly defeated at Culloden, and the *Young Pretender*, as he was called escaped to France after many adventures.

JOHN WESLEY (1703–1791)

John Wesley, with his brother, *Charles Wesley*, and *George Whitefield*, founded Methodism. They preached at great open-air meetings all over the country. John Wesley travelled 5,000 miles a year, on foot and on horseback, for fifty years, bringing religion and happiness to countless people, especially poor and humble folk.

WAR WITH FRANCE

The Seven Years' War with France lasted from 1756–1763. The year 1759 was known as the 'Year of

A Ship
at the time
of the Battle of
Quiberon Bay

Victories': *James Wolfe* captured Quebec and added Canada to the British Empire, *Admiral Hawke* destroyed the French Fleet at Quiberon Bay, and *Robert Clive* brought India under British rule.

THE AMERICAN COLONIES

In George III's reign the settlers in America, who at this time had mostly come from Britain, refused to pay taxes to the 'home' country and declared their Independence. Under the leadership of *George Washington*, and helped by the French, they defeated the British by 1783 and formed a new country: the United States of America.

THE WARS WITH NAPOLEON

After the French Revolution, which lasted from 1789 to 1793, the great general, *Napoleon Bonaparte*, led the French armies in their long struggle against Britain and her allies. *Nelson's* victory at Trafalgar (1805) saved England from invasion and gave her command of the seas. The *Duke of Wellington* wore down Napoleon's armies in Spain, and finally, with the Prussians under Blücher, defeated him at the battle of Waterloo (1815).

REFORMERS

The work of *John Wesley* led others to take an interest in the many poor and unfortunate people of these times.

John Howard and *Elizabeth Fry*, both Quakers, worked hard to improve the crowded and unhealthy prisons, and to give prisoners a chance to lead better lives.

William Wilberforce made people realise that slavery was shameful, and through his work the Slave Trade, by which negroes had been carried off from their homes in Africa and sold in America, was stopped in 1807. Slavery was forbidden in British Dominions in 1833 and all slaves were given their freedom.

Lord Shaftesbury did much to help children and the poor. His Factory Acts gradually reduced the long hours worked by women and children in factories, and prevented them from going down the coalmines. Shaftesbury carried on his work into Queen Victoria's reign, starting the Ragged Schools, helping the poor and supporting a law to forbid small boys working as chimney-sweeps.

1. TRAVEL

ROADS

Travel became popular in Georgian times, but the dreadful condition of the roads and the likelihood of meeting highwaymen made it very dangerous.

Sometimes ruts in the roads became so deep that travellers were hidden from view, and there were pot-holes where a man might drown on a dark night. In some places the road disappeared altogether, and it was necessary to hire a guide to reach the next town. In wet weather travellers hired teams of oxen to drag their coach out of the mud, while in summer the ruts were baked so hard that coaches sometimes turned off into the fields.

Each parish was supposed to look after its own roads, but little was done, and few people understood road-making. At last a plan was made to raise money to pay for repairs. Parliament allowed turnpikes and toll-gates on the busy roads, and travellers using the roads had to pay a toll, or fee, at each turnpike.

Hyde Park Corner Turnpike. Notice the posts marking the footpath, the milkmaid, and the stage-waggon.

ROAD-MAKERS

The first of the new road-makers was *John Metcalfe*, known as Blind Jack of Knaresborough. He was given

the job of laying three miles of turnpike road. He did it so well that he became a road-maker, and in time he laid over two hundred miles of road, mostly in Yorkshire.

A more famous road-maker was *Thomas Telford*, a Scottish engineer. He realised that roads must be well drained. The foundations of his roads were dug deep, and filled with large stones, followed by layers of smaller stones, which were well-rolled in. He built many roads, including the difficult Shrewsbury to Holyhead road. He also built the famous Menai Bridge.

Macadam Directing the Building of a New Road

Telford's methods were improved upon by *John Macadam*, another Scot, and the greatest road-maker of the time. Macadam said that deep digging and large stones were unnecessary. All that was needed was a layer, 25 to 30 centimetres deep, of small hard stones, not more than 25 millimetres long or wide. The iron-rimmed wheels of the coaches would grind a fine powder on top, which, washed down by rain, would bind the road together and keep it firm, but springy. People laughed at such a simple idea, until Macadam proved he was right. He was then put in charge of road-making in many parts of the country, and by 1840, 22,000 miles of new road had been laid, with 8,000 turnpikes to pay for their upkeep. It was noticed that coach horses, which in the old days had been worn out after three years, now lasted seven years on the macadamised roads.

THE STAGE-COACH

The most important vehicles on the new roads were the stage-coaches, which made regular runs between London and most large towns. They stopped at 'stages' along the road to put down and collect passengers, to change horses and to stay for the night at an inn.

The stage-coach was a heavy vehicle, pulled by four or six horses, and travelled at a steady five miles an hour. Inside the coach were two cushioned seats taking three persons on each side. Outside passengers travelled at a cheaper rate, either in the luggage basket which was slung between the back wheels, or on the roof, clinging to the baggage. It is difficult to say which was the more uncomfortable way of travelling.

About 1750, the coach which left London for Birmingham, starting at five o'clock in the morning, took two and a half days over the journey. Dover was a two-day journey, the passengers dining at Rochester and sleeping at Canterbury. Norwich was also two days' travelling distance, York was four and Exeter six. The long trip to Edinburgh took ten days in summer and twelve in winter. The cost of so many meals and lodgings on the way made travel expensive.

Horses were changed about every ten miles at the 'stages,' which were inns, each keeping a large number of horses for hire to the coach companies. While the horses were being changed in the yard, bustling with grooms, ostlers and postboys, the passengers had a chance to stretch their legs. In winter they warmed their numbed fingers and took a glass of ale or steaming punch at the inn's fireside.

CARRIAGES

There were many other vehicles to be seen on the roads besides the stagecoaches. The *post-chaise* ('chaise' is pronounced 'shays'), was lighter in build and faster than the stagecoach and had curved springs from which leather straps held the body. It was drawn by two

Post-chaise

or four horses, in charge of smart post-boys, who rode one to each pair of horses. Only well-to-do gentry could afford this way of travelling, which was considered to be much superior to travel by public stage-coach.

High Perch Phaeton

Lighter and faster still, was the *phaeton* ('fay-eton'), an open four-wheeled carriage drawn by one or two horses, which aristocratic travellers drove themselves.

Gig

A *gig* was a light two-wheeled cart pulled by one horse. A similar vehicle drawn by two horses was called a *curricle*, while a gig with a hood was a *cabriolet*, later known as a 'cab.' This began to take the place of the heavy hackney-coach in London streets, and its driver was always knows as 'cabby.'

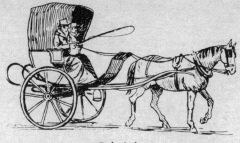

Cabriolet

The *landau* (pronounced 'lando'), named after a German town, was a coach with a hood which could be opened. A *whiskey* was a light gig, and a *sulky* was the charming name given to a little carriage for one person only.

Landau   Whiskey

THE STAGE-WAGGON

Strings of pack-horses laden with bundles of goods had not yet disappeared from the roads, and the huge *stage-waggons*, with their wide wheels and teams of eight and ten horses, continued to plod along at two or three miles an hour, to the annoyance of the coaches. Inside the waggons were as many as thirty or forty passengers, who could not afford stage-coach prices. They sat huddled together on bales of merchandise.

Stage-Waggon

THE MAIL-COACH

The finest of all the vehicles was the *mail-coach*. The first Royal Mail ran from Bath to London in 1784 and made the 106 miles journey in the record time of sixteen hours. As the roads improved, the mail-coach became the fastest vehicle of all, dashing along at a steady twelve miles an hour, carrying passengers and the precious bags of letters. Behind rode the guard with his musical horn, and a blunderbuss for use against highwaymen. The mail-coach had a change of horses every seven miles, so that it could keep up its speed.

Mail-Coach

The mail-coach drivers were the lords of the road, well-dressed, and often young and handsome. They drove their splendid horses with superb skill, to the envy of every boy along the road.

HIGHWAYMEN

With coaches now travelling at greater speeds, and with the cutting down of trees bordering the roads, which had given shelter, it was more difficult for Tobymen to ply their trade, and they became less numerous. Another disadvantage for robbers was that travellers now began to carry paper money instead of gold, and this could be traced.

But there were still a few daring highwaymen who worked alone or in small groups, the most famous being *Dick Turpin*, who was really a horse-thief and burglar.

There was *Captain Maclean*, the Gentleman Highwayman, with his elegant manners and respectable friends, and *Jack Rann*, who had been a coachman.

Jack Rann was known as 'Sixteen-string Jack' from his habit of wearing eight coloured laces at each knee of his breeches. He dressed in scarlet, with white silk stockings and laced hat. A bold and daring fellow, he boasted of his exploits. His boasting led to his downfall, and he was hanged at Newgate.

One famous hold-up took place in 1775, when the Norwich coach was waylaid in Epping Forest by seven highwaymen. The guard shot three of them dead with his blunderbuss before he was killed himself.

There were also many travellers who rode on horseback, from educated gentlemen who wished to see the countryside in their own way and at their own pace, to travelling pedlars on their bony hacks, taking ribbons, laces, combs and cotton goods into the villages. *John Wesley*, the great preacher, rode on horseback in all weathers, reading as he went.

If two companions had only one horse, they would journey in an amusing way called 'ride-and-tie.' One would start walking and the other would ride on ahead for a few miles, when he would dismount, tie the horse to a tree and proceed on foot. Presently his friend would reach the horse, untie it, mount and ride on until he had passed his companion by several miles. He would then dismount, tether the horse and walk on.

A Journey by Ride-and-Tie

Lastly, there were the poorest travellers, who made their way on foot, taking a lift on a stage-waggon when they could afford a few pence. These were the travelling players, jugglers, pedlars, journeymen and tinkers, and country lads trudging to London to seek their fortunes.

INNS

The inns and posthouses in the towns and villages along the main roads were as necessary to travellers as the coaches and horses. Some were splendid places, where the traveller was met by a smiling landlord and a host of servants, grooms and waiters, ready with hot drinks and well-cooked dinners. Their beds had snow-white linen and were aired by copper warming-pans. Such inns were for wealthy travellers. They took in only the 'quality,' gentry arriving in their own coaches or hired post-chaises. Others, which were far from comfortable, charged high prices for wretched food and dirty beds.

The Yard of a Busy Coaching Inn

Inns which accommodated stage-coach passengers would not admit waggon company, unless they went into the kitchen and ate with the servants. But the servants of gentlefolk thought themselves far superior to the poor. Putting on airs and graces, they copied their masters and mistresses, and demanded a separate room for supper.

As for the poor foot-traveller, everyone looked down on him and often the door was slammed in his face.

Servants shouted after him that a man who could not afford to travel in a better fashion might as well sleep under the hedge.

Waiters, chambermaids, grooms and postboys all expected a tip and their rudeness was well known if the tip was not large enough. The coach-driver received sixpence ($2\frac{1}{2}$p) from each passenger at the end of every stage.

THE GOLDEN AGE OF COACHING

In the last thirty years of the Georgian period (1800 to 1830) traffic increased in speed and numbers beyond anything which had ever been known. Over a thousand vehicles left London every day, using altogether about four thousand horses. Ten miles on, in all directions, and at stages all over the country, hundreds more horses were waiting to relieve them.

On Macadam's new roads travel by night became more common. The mail-coaches drove all day and night from every part of the kingdom, and arrived together at the Post Office in Lombard Street, London, at six o'clock in the morning.

The stage-coaches ran faster and faster, and the sight of them, varnished and shining, their splendid horses driven by skilful coachmen, filled men with excitement and pleasure. Some men, indeed, spent much of their time riding in any new coach, on any fast run, for the sheer joy of it.

The coachmen, if not quite so glorious as the mail-coach drivers, were lordly figures in their low-brimmed hats, striped waistcoats, topboots and huge driving coats, as they swaggered into the inn-yards, and took a glass of hot grog.

Their coaches all had names: *Magnet, Comet, Express, Lightning, Greyhound* and *Rocket*, and each had its rival belonging to another company, which would race neck and neck along Macadam's smooth roads. Speed was everything, and the drivers took a pride in arriving punctually at every stage.

A Stage-Coach Well Ahead of its Rival

As the coach drew near to its inn the guard sounded his horn. Fresh horses were brought out ready and were changed with all speed. There was time now only for a bite of food and a hasty pull at a mug of ale before the coach was off again.

Traffic grew so great that at Hounslow, for instance, a famous coaching centre near London, with many inns, 2,500 horses were kept for posting. Large inns could stable as many as six hundred horses.

The Old Bell Inn, Holborn

On May-day each year the coaches and horses were decked with ribbons and flowers, and at Christmas with sprigs of holly, while the coachmen wore enormous buttonholes, and tied bows on their whips.

A Coach on May-day

This, then, was the Glorious Age of Coaching, the time when the coaches, the Royal Mail, the post-chaises, and all those oddly named vehicles already mentioned, drove down the road in a cloud of dust and splendour. But this glory came to a sudden end.

The railways arrived. In ten or fifteen years, by tremendously hard work, a network of railway lines spread all over the country. Train travel was cheaper, as one train could carry more passengers than thirty coaches. The coaches, the lordly inns and the host of drivers, grooms and servants were ruined.

TOWN TRAVEL IN GEORGIAN DAYS

The most elegant form of travel for short journeys, in the eighteenth century, was by *sedan chair*.

In days when rich and fashionable people wore silk clothes and astonishingly high hair styles, they needed some convenient form of transport through the narrow and muddy streets. They hired sedan chairs and were carried to the assembly or ball by two burly chairmen. The nobility had their own richly ornamented sedans, which stood in the lobby of their great homes, waiting until her ladyship was ready to go visiting.

Shillibeer's Omnibus

Horse-drawn vehicles were used in the town for many years, and in 1829 a man named *Shillibeer* started the first *omnibus*. It was drawn by three horses and ran from the City to a public-house on the Edgware Road called 'The Yorkshire Stingo.' As you can see, passengers were only carried inside.

Soon after the first trains, there appeared strange monsters driven by steam, called *steam-coaches*, which had been invented by a Frenchman named *Cugnot*. They caused alarm lest the boilers burst, but because of their novelty, they soon did a good trade. One man ran a

Scene Outside a London Coffee-House

service to Bath, but, after a while, a law was passed forcing these vehicles off the roads, and allowing only horse-drawn traffic.

A Steam-Coach

In 1810 the first bicycle, again a French invention, appeared in England. It was known as the *hobby horse*, or *dandy horse*, and was built partly of wood and partly of iron. The rider swung his legs so that his toes touched the ground and pushed him along. The hobby horse

soon went out of fashion, and fifty years passed before
the *boneshaker* made its appearance.

A Hobby Horse

2. SHIPS AND SAILORS

During this period, Britain was building up her trade and increasing her Empire overseas. Her strength lay, not in the Army, but in the Royal Navy. Throughout the long wars with France many famous sea-battles, such as the battle of the Nile and the battle of Trafalgar, took place.

A Warship of the Mid-Eighteenth Century

THE PRESS GANG

In spite of the great importance of the Royal Navy, life on board His Majesty's ships was so hard that no man would willingly serve as an ordinary seaman unless he wished to escape from a crime or debt.

The sailors' food was foul and often unfit to eat. They had no fresh vegetables, so scurvy was a common disease. Their sleeping quarters were cramped and unhealthy. Pay was scanty and often in arrears, yet discipline was iron-hard and brutal in the extreme.

When sailors were needed for the Navy, they were usually obtained by force of the Press Gang. In seafaring towns a party of sailors, led by an officer and all armed with cutlasses, would enter the taverns, shops and markets to seize any likely-looking man and carry him off to serve as a seaman.

Mariners and fishermen were taken from peaceful ships in harbour, merchant ships returning from voyages were often boarded on their way up Channel to London, husbands were snatched from their work and, it is said, a bridegroom and many of the congregation were once carried off from the church door!

Sailors in the Navy at this time had no official uniform, but the mark of a seaman was his thick, short pig-tail, which stood out, because it was stiffened with tar or grease.

Naval Officers

Naval officers were no longer nobles from the Court, as in Charles II's time. Usually they were younger sons of

The *Royal George* at Deptford and the launching of the *Cambridge*
(from a painting of 1757)

gentlemen, who were sent to sea under the eye of a captain. They started with the rank of midshipman, and learned the art of seamanship the hard way.

Conditions in the Navy were so bad that there were serious mutinies during the French wars. Yet these ill-fed, ill-paid ruffians were the magnificent seamen who fought and died with Hawke and Nelson. There is little doubt that they were the finest sailors in the world.

SHIPS

The *Royal George*, a ship of 2,000 tons, is a fine example of an eighteenth-century ship. She was built at Woolwich in 1756 and was equipped with a hundred guns. She had the old-fashioned beaked bows and lanterns on her poop. She carried a bowsprit sail and a triangular lateen sail on the mizzen mast.

The *Victory* at Sea

Nelson's flagship, The *Victory*, was of much the same size: 2,162 tons and 57 metres long, and she was manned by a crew of 830 men. Her bows were not beaked, but were built as part of the hull.

In Nelson's day she carried 102 guns, a mixture of 42-, 24- and 12-pounders which had a range of 350 to 550 metres. The guns blazed round shot and grape shot at the crowded decks of the ships they attacked, while sharp-shooters in the rigging picked off officers.

Sea-battles, such as Trafalgar, were fought at close quarters, and after several broadsides from the guns, boarding parties swarmed on to the enemy ships. When a ship was disabled or had lost so many of her crew that she could no longer navigate, she hauled down her flag and surrendered.

Merchant ships were far more numerous than warships. There were the West Indiamen, fast low sloops of about 400 tons, which were known as 'slavers.'

A West Indiaman

West Indiamen carried cotton goods from Liverpool to West Africa, exchanged them for slaves to take to the West Indies, and came home with a cargo of fruit, sugar and rum. These fast ships were sometimes seized by mutinous crews and became pirate vessels, which, from their hideouts among the islands of the West Indies, preyed upon peaceful merchant shipping.

The great East Indiamen, engaged on trade with India and the Far East, were slower ships. They were well-armed against pirates and against the French. They carried provisions for the long voyage round the Cape of Good Hope, lasting six months, and often were away from home for a year or more.

An East Indiaman

THE FIRST STEAMSHIP

On the sea, as well as on land, the age of steam was approaching. Nelson realised that steam warships must one day replace his wooden *Victory*, but it was still many years before the Navy went over to steam.

In 1802, after some years of experiment, a Scotsman named *William Symington* built a steam engine to drive a tugboat called the *Charlotte Dundas*. Her trials on a canal were most successful, but the canal-owners were afraid that the wash from her paddle-wheel would injure the canal banks, and she was never used again.

Drawing of Symington's First Steamboat 1789

Thus, *Henry Bell's Comet* of 1812 was the first steamship in regular service. She was a small ship with one 4-horse-power engine and a sail on her tall funnel. On her trips along the Scottish coast she reached the great speed of $7\frac{1}{2}$ miles per hour.

The *Comet* 1812

By 1821 steamers were making regular crossings between Dover and Calais, and men were talking of building iron ships. But these did not come for some time, and sailing ships still had a long and glorious age before them.

SMUGGLERS

High taxes upon tea, silk and such French goods as wine, brandy and lace made smuggling a flourishing trade in the eighteenth century. People regarded smuggling as an almost innocent occupation, like poaching. The smugglers found it easy to supply the gentry with tea and brandy and their ladies with lace, silk and gloves, on which not a penny tax had been paid.

All along the coast, and especially in Kent and Sussex, smuggling was a regular trade, and the boatmen were helped by the local people. Goods were brought ashore at night from French boats or from homeward bound

East Indiamen and were hidden in barns, cellars and even churches, until they could be safely taken to London. There were many desperate fights with the Customs Officers, for smugglers who were caught might be hanged or transported to a convict colony abroad.

CANALS

For a long time the rivers had carried considerable traffic, chiefly because the roads were so badly kept and waggons were slow. In the first half of the eighteenth century many rivers were deepened and widened, and locks were built so that barges could be raised or lowered to different water levels.

James Brindley

In the middle of the century came the great period of canal-making. *The Duke of Bridgewater* and his engineer, *James Brindley*, built a canal from Worsley to

Manchester, to carry coal from the Duke's mines. It was realised at once that here was a way of sending heavy goods from one place to another more quickly and cheaply than by slow-moving waggons on the roads.

Barton Bridge, showing how Brindley carried a Canal over a River

Large gangs of rough labourers dug out the canal-beds and constructed bridges and aqueducts, which took the waterways across the countryside. These labourers were called 'navvies,' short for 'navigators,' since the canals were built for 'inland navigation.'

The Manchester-Liverpool Canal was followed by the Grand Junction Canal, which joined the rivers Mersey and Trent, and soon a whole network of canals linking up the rivers spread all over England.

All our present canals, with the exception of the Manchester Ship Canal, had been built by 1830, and most of them are still in use.

3. HOUSES IN GEORGIAN DAYS

Much of the wealth which came from our increasing trade and from the new methods of farming was spent on building fine houses in both town and country.

Perhaps the new houses did not have the warm friendliness of Tudor homes, but they were stately and noble. Many of them were designed in the style of Roman temples.

A Large House Built in the Classical Style

Great houses, such as Buckingham House and Blenheim Palace, were built with a splendid central block to which the kitchens on the one side and stables on the other were connected by a colonnade.

These great houses had magnificent rooms for assemblies and balls, richly decorated with statues, pillars and huge oil paintings in gilt frames.

The Hall of a Great Georgian House

The ceilings and walls were covered with plaster designs and pictures, usually in the Italian style. The furnishings were lavish and elegant, and were often modelled on the new ideas brought home from abroad by the young lords.

Robert Adam, a popular architect of this time, designed many of the lofty drawing-rooms in these great houses in his own style.

Many of his rooms had curved ceilings, and plaster decorations in delicate shades of pink, green and blue. They were often rounded at one end.

The Library at The Iveagh Bequest, Kenwood, London, known as The Adam Room

Wooden panelling began to go out of fashion, and hand-painted wallpaper took its place.

The fireplace of white marble had its coal fire in a raised, decorated grate, while above it was a gilt-framed mirror between silver candlesticks. Elaborate glass chandeliers were used for lighting.

At its best, this style had a noble dignity, and it suited the aristocrats, with their rich clothes, their powdered wigs and fine manners.

A town house in Georgian days

Georgian houses of moderate size were perhaps the most pleasant-looking houses ever built. Many of them are still to be seen in the older parts of our towns.

The outside was usually plain and simple, of red brick or white stucco, with sash windows and a handsome doorway.

The roof was tiled and had dormer windows, but no gables. Attached to the wrought-iron railings in front of the house was a metal cone.

Here the linkboy, after lighting her ladyship home at night, doused his flaming torch.

Inside these homes of well-to-do gentlefolk were comfortable rooms, lit by tall windows and furnished with carpets, rugs and graceful chairs. The furnishings were elegant, but they were not as extravagant as those in the great houses.

A Georgian Bedroom with its Four-poster Bed

Candles had long been the only means of lighting, but now lamps, which burned a fine whale-oil, began to replace them.

Many of the London squares and crescents belong to this period. Some of them were built by *John Nash*, a famous architect, whose liking for plaster and stucco caused this rhyme.

"But is not our Nash too a very great Master,
He finds us all brick and leaves us all plaster."

A London Square

In the poorer parts were still to be found narrow, filthy alleys, with old overhanging houses.

GARDENS

Even the gardens and grounds of the great country houses were designed in a new style and were very different from the trim Tudor and Stuart gardens, with their clipped hedges, square flower beds and straight paths.

The fashionable idea was to bring the natural countryside right up to the big house and, at the same time, to provide a fine view down a wide avenue of trees.

Immense sums of money were spent in laying out parks with artificial lakes and fountains, raised mounds, terraces and statues, pavilions and summer-houses, as well as clumps of trees and shrubs.

William Kent

The experts in this 'landscape' gardening were *William Kent* and *'Capability' Brown*, an odd character, who gained his name from his habit of always saying he saw "capability of improvement" in an estate.

"Capability" Brown

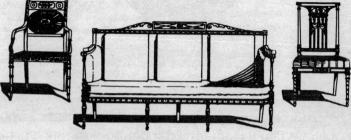

Sheraton Furniture

FURNITURE

Georgian furniture became elegant and costly. The sturdy oak of earlier times gave place to more ornamental woods, such as walnut, beech and mahogany, and we begin to hear of chairs and tables being made in various styles, named after their makers.

Chippendale Furniture

The most famous names in furniture-making were *Chippendale*, *Hepplewhite* and *Sheraton*, who were three designers of furniture at this time. Examples of their work can still be seen today. *Hepplewhite* made his

Hepplewhite Furniture

chairs, tables and sideboards more delicately than
Chippendale, and for decoration he often used inlay
patterns of different coloured woods. *Sheraton* made
some beautiful furniture, but it was sometimes rather
fussy and over-ornamented.

Adam Furniture

Our trade with the East brought fresh ideas and new
materials. Furniture was made of cane and bamboo,
and Chinese patterns and designs were copied.

There was now more furniture in the houses than in
Stuart times, and it was comfortably upholstered.
Curtains, bed-hangings and cushions were made of
wonderfully patterned materials, for rich people
wanted their homes to be decorative as well as useful.

English Pottery and Porcelain

There was a new interest in vases, statues and pottery, much of it in Greek and Roman styles.

Pianos were invented by an Italian in 1709 and they gradually took the place of the spinet. It is said that the best violins were made in the eighteenth century.

THEIR CLOTHES

A Georgian gentleman wore a waisted coat, stiffened to make the skirts stand out. His wide cuffs were turned back to show the white shirt underneath and he wore a cravat at his throat.

Wigs were usually tied behind, and for special occasions they were powdered and curled. When indoors, gentlemen wore a kind of turban or nightcap over their shaven heads. Three-cornered hats were. popular, but they were no longer decorated with feathers.

How Gentlemen Wore their Hair

There was not so much lace worn as in Charles II's time and men's clothes were not of such bright colours. From this time onward they gradually became quieter and duller.

Men carried snuff boxes, since smoking was now considered a low habit, fit only for sailors and workmen.

Ladies' dresses were made of heavy, rich materials, and their skirts were either stretched over hoops or stiffened with whalebone.

Their hair was worn in curls and ringlets, with a little lace cap, or a large straw hat on top. Every lady of fashion carried a fan with a jewelled handle.

By the end of the eighteenth century ladies were wearing wigs and false hair, powdered and curled, and piled up into enormous shapes over small cushions.

Imitation fruit, flowers and even ships were added as ornaments. A tax on powder put an end to this odd fashion.

At the turn of the century there were many changes in dress. Gone were the heavy silks and rich brocades.

Dresses, as you can see in the picture above, were now made of flimsy muslin and lawn. They became very simple, and followed the style of the ancient Greeks.

Men's coats became tight-waisted and had cutaway tails.

The picture below [about 1815] shows the great change which occurred in men's dress; trousers became fashionable in place of knee-breeches, which were only worn by old gentlemen and on certain occasions at Court.

At Brighton, *Beau Brummell*, prince of the dandies, was leading the fashion for the 'bucks,' as gay young men were called. His dress included padded shoulders, tight waists (some men wore corsets), starched neckcloths and very tight trousers.

CHILDREN

Until Georgian times, children were dressed exactly like their parents, but now they began to have their own styles. The fashion for girls to wear long drawers down to their ankles, called pantaloons, lasted for many years.

SOLDIERS

The army became more popular during Wellington's struggle with the French. Laurel-decked coaches often carried the news of his victories to town and village.

Grenadier—1746   Footsoldier—1746

The ordinary soldiers in the Army were the lowest, roughest men in the land, for only crime, drink or unemployment would make a man join the ranks. Wellington called them "the scum of the earth," though he added they made "fine fellows" in the end. The discipline of the sergeants was very hard, and punishment was usually the lash. Yet in battle the British troops proved to be among the finest in Europe.

Guardsman at the time of Waterloo

An Officer in 1756

Trooper 23rd Dragoons 1809

The officers were sons of lords and rich men who bought their places for large sums of money, and looked on soldiering as an expensive hobby.

Even in the long war against Napoleon, they continued to dress like dandies, to attend balls and to go hunting. Wellington found some of them putting up umbrellas in battle to protect their fine uniforms!

The uniforms of this period were brightly coloured: red coats, white breeches and black boots. In time, the full-skirted coat with wide cuffs changed to a cut-away jacket. Hats and caps varied according to regiments.

Ordinary soldiers were paid only two or three shillings (about 10p to 15p) a week, but prices were low. They could get drunk for very little. Their lives were rough and hard, but they had to keep their uniforms trim.

WEAPONS

Swords, cutlasses and daggers went out of fashion in the Army, except for officers and cavalry. The ordinary soldier relied on his musket and bayonet. His musket was a heavy gun weighing 7 kilogrammes, which must have been tiring to carry on long marches. Soldiers marched everywhere and often went into action after a night march of ten or fifteen miles. Gunpowder charges were carried in paper packets, called cartridges, but the flint, which lasted for about twenty shots, was useless in the rain.

A musket was accurate up to fifty or a hundred metres, so the troops fought in two ranks, the front rank kneeling down. When all fired together, it was called a volley. Our troops were famous for holding their fire until the enemy was very near. They then fired a volley and followed it up with a bayonet charge. After a halt, they reformed their ranks and reloaded.

The cannons, or artillery, were mounted on wheels or gun carriages and pulled by horses. They fired round-shot, cannon balls and shrapnel a distance of about half a mile.

Cannon at the battle of Waterloo

5. THE PEOPLE'S WORK

ENCLOSURES

All through Georgian times, tremendous changes were taking place in the country districts.

For hundreds of years the land had been farmed in open fields, divided into strips, which the farmers and peasants rented from the Lord of the Manor. The poor countryman eked out his living by keeping a few animals, geese, ducks or chickens on the common-land, and also by spinning and weaving in his cottage.

Country Folk in the Eighteenth Century

The big landowners now wanted to get rid of this strip-farming, so that larger farms could be made and more efficient methods of farming used. Parliament passed a law whereby the landowner could force the peasant to give up his strip of land, in exchange for a few pounds, or for some land, which was usually poorer, in another part of the estate.

Hedges were planted and the land was divided into fields. Sometimes several fields were let out as farms to farmers with money of their own, but they were charged a higher rent than before. The owner farmed the rest of the land himself. Gradually the common-land was enclosed too, the woods were cut down and neat plantations of trees took their place.

These new farms grew larger quantities of corn than the strips had done. Prices were high owing to the wars with France, and the landowners and farmers made their fortunes.

Cultivator for Surface Weeds

Wiltshire Plough over a Hundred Years Old

NEW METHODS OF FARMING

Instead of leaving fields to lie fallow for a year, *Lord Townshend* (often known as 'Turnip' Townshend), began growing turnips, to be used in winter for cattle and sheep fodder. Better grass was grown for hay, and it was no longer necessary to kill off nearly all the cattle in autumn, and to salt down their flesh.

Fresh meat could now be bought in winter, which meant that the disease called scurvy became less common and the people's health improved.

Thomas Coke, who lived at Holkham in Norfolk, improved his land by careful farming, and produced a fine breed of sheep. People came from all over England and Europe to see his fine animals, and to watch the Holkham sheep-shearings.

Walker's Galleries   Coke of Norfolk

Robert Bakewell of Leicestershire also greatly improved the quality of his farm animals, and other farmers tried to do the same. The animals at Smithfield Meat Market doubled in weight during the eighteenth century.

Smithfield Market, London

Jethro Tull, in Queen Anne's reign, had invented a machine which sowed corn in neat rows. The seed was spread evenly and the land could be weeded and hoed between the rows of young shoots.

This new method of sowing, which took the place of scattering by hand, together with new ideas about manuring, produced heavier crops. Tull also invented a simple threshing machine; a number of sticks were set in motion, and they beat out the corn from the ear.

POOR COUNTRYFOLK

Poor countryfolk found that the few pounds paid to them for their land did not last very long. Some managed to buy another small piece of land, but even so, life was difficult for them. They had lost the common-land, where a cow, a pig or two and some geese had been kept. The woods, which had given them firewood and an occasional hare or rabbit, were cut down or guarded by gamekeepers with guns and steel traps.

Another change was taking place. With the coming of machines and factories, spinning and weaving in the cottages was dying out. The peasants, distressed and angry, went off to the towns to look for work in the new factories. Often there was no work for men, but only for women and children, who were paid a lower wage than a man.

If he was fortunate, a peasant might find work on a farm as a labourer for a shilling (5p) a day. This was not enough to feed his family upon, so his wife worked in the fields also. When the price of bread rose very high, he was given a little money from the poor rates.

WORK IN THE TOWNS

In the days of the Stuarts and in the times of George I and George II, nearly everything that ordinary people needed, clothes, tools, bread, meat and beer, was made in their own villages. Only the wealthy sent to London for books, furniture, china and such fine things.

By the end of the Georgian age, new 'manufacturing' towns had sprung up near the coalmines and iron industry, mostly in the Midlands and North of England. People now worked together in large numbers, in factories, instead of at home with their families.

INVENTORS

Spinning is the process of making raw wool or cotton, after it has been carded, into a thread. This was done for hundreds of years by hand-spinning, and later with a spinning-wheel.

Weaving is the process of making the spun thread into cloth by passing a shuttle in and out between cross threads, like darning. For many years this had been done on a machine worked by one weaver, who threw the shuttle from one hand to the other.

Hargreaves' Spinning Jenny

In 1733 a certain *James Kay* invented a Flying Shuttle which made weaving so quick that faster spinning was needed to keep up with the weavers. By 1764 *James Hargreaves*, himself a poor weaver, through watching his wife Jenny at her wheel, was able to perfect a spinning machine which kept pace with the weavers. He called it his Spinning Jenny.

Next, *Richard Arkwright*, a barber, who listened to talk about machines while on his way round the mills selling wigs, made a spinning-machine, worked not by hand, but by water-power. *Samuel Crompton* made an even better machine called a Mule, and spinning went ahead of weaving.

Carding, Drawing and Roving

Later came steam-power, which really caused factories to take the place of cottage work. *James Watt's* name is always linked with early steam-engines, but he was not the inventor. He was an instrument-maker in Glasgow, who one day was asked to repair an early steam-engine.

An Industrial Town in the North of England

A man called *Newcomen* is said to have made the first steam-engine. Watt saw its faults and began to work on a better model. He found a partner in *Mathew Boulton* of Birmingham, and together they set up a factory there. By 1781 they had made a steam-engine which could be used to drive machinery.

A Clergyman, the *Rev. Edmund Cartwright*, now invented a weaving loom driven by one of these steam-engines. This new way of driving machines was quickly used for flour, silk, cotton and saw-mills.

Power Loom Weaving

Factories were built and fitted with these new machines, and thread and cloth were produced more quickly and cheaply than by the old methods. Unemployed folk from the country came to work in the factories, and rows of cheap, shoddily built houses were put up for them, as near to the factories as possible. No thought was given to fresh air, water supply, beauty or cleanliness, and they soon became slums.

Back-to-Back Slums

As the population was growing, there were plenty of workers wanting jobs, so wages were low and hours of work very long. Men could not earn enough, so their little children at the age of six or seven years went to work all day in the factories with them. If they grew tired they were beaten awake by the 'strapper'; if they went to sleep they often fell into the machinery and were injured or killed.

Cloth was produced very cheaply at this time, and as trade increased, the mill-owners became very rich, but most of the workers remained poor and miserable. Only a very few were able to save enough money to start factories of their own.

Children at Work in a Cotton Mill

Of course it must not be thought that all the working people of England were suddenly forced into factories and slums.

Most of the skilled trades continued to flourish in the small workshops of the towns and villages: the clockmakers, tailors, blacksmiths, harnessmakers, carpenters and coachbuilders were craftsmen who could do their work far better than machines. The hosts of servants in big houses and inns, the ostlers, grooms and all those engaged in the coaching business, the farmworkers and the fisherfolk had never heard of the dark, gloomy factories in the North of England.

6. THE PEOPLE AT PLAY IN GEORGIAN ENGLAND

The sports and pastimes of Stuart England were cruel and bloodthirsty, and although the Georgian Age was less savage, many of the same sports were carried on, for people do not change their ways suddenly. There were still the old Bankside sports of *bull and bear baiting, sword-fights* and *cock-fighting*.

An advertisement of this time says:

> "A mad bull to be dressed up with fireworks and turned loose. A dog to be dressed up with fireworks all over and turned loose with the bull. Also a bear to be turned loose and a cat to be tied to the bull's tail."

Sword-fights between fencing masters were very popular and were given before large crowds, who were disappointed if one of the fencers was not seriously wounded.

Fighting a Duel

This was the age of *duels*. To settle a dispute, gentlemen would "call each other out" to fight with swords or pistols. A wound usually ended the duel, but men were sometimes killed.

Prize-fighting, with bare knuckles, was the forerunner of modern boxing. Fights were held in the open air and lasted 50, 60 or even 100 rounds.

Prize-fights were forbidden by law, but as they were so popular with the gentlemen of fashion, who betted on the winner, they took place regularly in fields and commons just outside London. When the news went round that a contest was to be held, all the roads leading to the spot were thronged with every kind of cart, chaise, coach and carriage, jostling their way to the match.

Cock-fighting, as you can see in this picture, *horse-racing* and even *donkey-racing* for the chimney-sweeps, were excuses for gambling; people would even bet on such odd contests as pudding- or tripe-eating matches!

A Print Published in 1743, Showing a Game of Cricket

Cricket now became a popular team game, with recognised rules. As early as 1744 Kent played All-England and beat them by 111 notches to 110. The score was kept by cutting a notch on a stick for each

The Cock-Pit

run. On page 71 you can see the early wicket and club-like bat. By 1830 three stumps and a broad bat were in use, and round-arm bowling was taking the place of underarm bowling.

FAIRS

The great London fair, St. Bartholomew's at Smithfield, was still held every year, with its stalls, sideshows, wrestling and merry-go-rounds. By 1800 it had become so rowdy and such a lawless nuisance that it was decided it should be held no longer.

There were several other fairs, including Lady Fair at Southwark, which is shown in this amusing picture by *Hogarth*.

On the left, a stage is collapsing on to an ale-booth, though the actress with the drum continues to advertise the show. There is another show just starting at the back, a flying man, a peep-show in the foreground and a fencing master on horseback.

HUNTING

The games and amusements mentioned so far were those which everyone could enjoy, but there were other amusements for the 'gentry,' the large number of aristocrats and well-to-do folk who had plenty of money from their estates or factories. *Hunting* was their favourite outdoor sport. Deer hunts were now rare, but fox-hunting, with all the added excitement and skill of jumping hedges, took their place. The older sport of hunting the hare was even more popular, since a hare does not run so far afield as a fox.

Vauxhall Gardens

THE LONDON SEASON

One of the chief events of the year was *The London Season,* when the country gentry came up to spend a few weeks in London. They hired houses in a fasionable part of the town and brought their sons, daughters and servants with them. They came to see the sights and to enter the fashionable world at the assemblies, dances and balls which were given every night.

Playing Cards
Notice the Small Black Servant in the Background

Other places had their 'season' also. The most famous were Tunbridge Wells and Bath, to which the gentry went to drink the waters for their health, and to meet their friends for gossip and to enjoy themselves.

BATH

Bath was the most fashionable town in England. The baths made by the Romans were still in use, and these became popular in Stuart and Georgian times. In the eighteenth century the town was rebuilt in the new elegant style, and it remains to-day a wonderful example of Georgian building.

Drinking in the magnificent Pump Room gradually became more popular than bathing. But the beauties and the dandies came not only to drink the waters; they came to dance at the balls, to show off their clothes and to be taught the perfection of elegant behaviour by the lord and master of Bath – *Beau Nash,* the best dressed man in England.

A Dandy

On page 75 a delightful picture shows you the bath and its occupants in Charles II's reign. Round the cross in the middle were seats for the gentlemen, while round the walls were contained arches for ladies. Everyone sat in the warm water up to their necks.

At Bath, as at Tunbridge Wells, the gaming table was a centre of attraction. Hazard and faro were played, and, in later years, whist. Large fortunes and estates were sometimes gambled away in a night.

SEASIDE RESORTS

Although we are a seafaring people, it is strange that no one had thought of bathing in the sea until this time. In fact, people rarely even visited the seaside until Georgian days, when it suddenly became fashionable to visit the new seaside resorts of Brighton, Weymouth, Scarborough and Margate. People bathed from curious little bathing huts on wheels, which were pulled by horses to the water.

The Prince Regent at Brighton

When he was Prince Regent, George IV was very fond of Brighton. He spent much time there, and built an elaborate house in the style of an Eastern Palace which is known as the Pavilion.

COFFEE-HOUSES

Coffee-houses were still popular with citizens, merchants, writers, lawyers and clergymen. They all had their favourite house at which they called every morning to chat, to drink and to hear the latest news. For a penny they could borrow a newspaper.

At one time there were three thousand of these coffee-houses in London. *Doctor Johnson*, the writer and maker of the famous Dictionary, was well known for his conversation, and men crowded round him in the coffee-houses to listen to his talk on every subject.

The nobility now began to meet at Clubs instead of at the coffee-houses.

Dr. Johnson in his Coffee-house

NEWSPAPERS

For a long time there had been newsletters such as *The Spectator* and *The Tatler*, which gave the happenings of the day. News could also be heard in the coffee-houses, and at one of them *Edward Lloyd* became famous for his daily news about ships.

By George III's reign, printed newspapers appeared regularly at twopence and threepence each (about 1p). They had four pages and included news about Parliament, letters, poetry and advertisements.

The oldest newspaper, Berrow's *Worcester Journal* appeared in 1690. *The Daily Courant* (1702) was the first daily, and the *Evening Post* (1705) the first evening paper. Other early papers were the *Morning Post* and *The Times* (1785), but their price was too high for the ordinary citizen, so many people would share a paper between them.

7. THE STREETS IN GEORGIAN DAYS

The streets were roughly paved and without kerbstones, and posts protected the pathway, on which the chairmen were forbidden to carry their sedan chairs. Foul water and refuse ran down the middle of the road in a gutter. Signboards hung outside every house, announcing who lived there. Bow-windows, steps and porches jutted out into the path.

The noise of the street-criers, the bawling of the apprentices and shopkeepers, "Rally, ladies, rally! Buy! Buy! Buy!", the rumble of heavy carts and coaches, the shouts and quarrelling of the waggoners made a terrific din in the streets, to which was added the confusion caused by droves of animals going to be slaughtered.

"Buy a Rabbit"

"Fine Duke Cherries"

Even so, the streets were better than in Mr. Pepys's time, though the London mob could still terrify all law-abiding citizens, and bands of young nobles who called themselves 'Mohocks' made the streets dangerous at night by their rowdy behaviour. They insulted passers-by, tipped over sedan chairs, tripped up the Watch and assaulted the 'Charlies.'

"Buy a Fine Table Basket"

Besides the respectable tradesmen, workers and street sellers, there were hordes of poor and destitute who seldom had regular work, but lived as best they could. Thieving, robbery and murder were common crimes and punishments were savage. A man could be hanged for any one of two hundred crimes, such as sheep-stealing, pocket-picking, or, indeed, for any theft above five shillings (25p).

A public hanging was an entertainment which attracted huge crowds, who accompanied the condemned wretch through the streets with cheers and songs, or waited all night, enjoying themselves, outside Newgate Prison.

Street lighting, with oil lamps, made the way safer at night, while gas lamps, which appeared in 1807, excited great astonishment.

The New Gas Lamps in Pall Mall, London

THE POLICE

There was much crime in these days, for the old watchmen were feeble and frightened, and the chances of arrest were small. In 1780 the mob burned down seventy houses and four prisons. There were no police to stop them and the soldiers had to be called out.

The forerunners of our modern police were the Bow Street Runners. They were started by *Henry Fielding*, a magistrate at the Bow Street court. The Bow Street Runners wore red waistcoats and were often called Robin Redbreasts.

A Bow Street Runner

They were a detective force rather than policemen, for their jobs were to raid gambling houses, to pursue robbers and highwaymen and to track down murderers and wanted criminals. Unlike our police to-day, they were armed with pistols.

In 1829 the place of the Bow Street Runners was taken by the Metropolitan Police. Under *Sir Robert Peel* a body of three thousand men was recruited to bring law and order to London. Every part of London was patrolled by a policeman in uniform.

The first policemen wore top hats, blue coats, leather belts and white trousers, and each carried a truncheon and a rattle, which was used to call for extra help.

Quelling a Riot in 1844

At first the "Bobbies" or "Peelers," as they were called, were regarded with suspicion and they were jeered at, but sensible citizens soon realised the value of their work. The streets became safer than ever before.

A Peeler

PART TWO

IN THE REIGN OF
QUEEN VICTORIA

The Young Queen

SOME OF THE CHIEF EVENTS

Victoria reigned from 1837 to 1901. She married her cousin, *Prince Albert*, in 1840.

During her long reign, her chief ministers were *Peel, Palmerston, Salisbury, Gladstone* and *Disraeli*.

1840—*Sir Rowland Hill* started the Penny Post. Railways were being built all over Britain. Hunger and poverty was widespread, but trade was increasing.

1851— Prince Albert organised The Great Exhibition, housed in the Crystal Palace in Hyde Park. British goods were shown to visitors from all over the world.

1854–1856 The Crimean War was fought by Britain and France, against Russia. *Florence Nightingale*, by nursing the wounded, began her life's work for hospitals.

1857—The Indian Mutiny.

1865—*Lister*, a famous surgeon, was using antiseptics.

1869—Opening of the Suez Canal.

1870—The Education Act, compelling all children to attend school.

1850–1900 Until Victoria's reign little was known about the interior of Africa, but the discoveries of *Speke* and *Burton*, and the explorations of *David Livingstone* and an American journalist, *H. M. Stanley*, opened up the 'Dark Continent.' *Cecil Rhodes* founded Rhodesia and added vast lands to the Empire.

1899–1902 The South African War was fought between the Dutch settlers (Boers) and the British *Lord Kitchener* and *Baden-Powell*, who later founded the Boy Scouts, made their names in this war.

Throughout this reign there were a great many inventions and engineering triumphs. The chief of these were:

1838—Two steamships crossed the Atlantic in nineteen days.

1838—The first telegraph service in England was set up by *Wheatstone* and *Cooke*.

1858—The first trans-Atlantic cable was laid.

1862—The first London trams (horsedrawn).

1863—London's Underground Railway was opened.

1869—The 'boneshaker' bicycle appeared.

1876—*Bell's* first telephone (in Boston, U.S.A.).

1878—First public telephone exchange in London.

1880—First cargoes of frozen meat from abroad.

1884—*Daimler's* motor-car engine.

1885—*Benz* made the first motor-car (in Germany). *Stanley's* Safety Bicycle.

1888—*Dunlop's* air-filled tyres.

1897—*Marconi* and *Oliver Lodge* experimenting with wireless in London.

1901—*Marconi* received the first Trans-Atlantic wireless signal.

There were many famous writers in Victoria's reign, of whom *Charles Dickens* was the most popular.

1837—Pickwick Papers.

1848—David Copperfield.

Of the children's books, two of the most famous were:

1866—Alice in Wonderland.

1883—Treasure Island.

The Crystal Palace

8. THE COMING OF THE RAILWAYS

The arrival of the railways brought the Golden Age of Coaching to a sudden end.

For a number of years trucks had been used in the coalmining districts of the North of England and South Wales. They ran on wooden rails and carried coal down to the canals and rivers, and to the coalships bound for London.

By 1810 iron rails were in use, because they did not wear out so quickly as wooden ones.

Cugnot's Steam Carriage

STEAM-ENGINES

The first steam-engine which really worked was built by *Thomas Newcomen* in 1712 and was used to pump water out of a Cornish tin-mine. *James Watt* greatly improved this model, so that steam power could be used to drive machinery in factories and mills.

Such steam-engines were fixtures, and no self-moving engine had been invented until *Nicholas Cugnot*, a young Frenchman, built this curious monster called a steam carriage. Great crowds gathered to see him drive it in the streets of Paris.

Cugnot reached the amazing speed of nine miles an hour when the carriage overturned. This so alarmed the French people that Cugnot and his machine were locked up.

As far as we know, *William Murdoch*, an engineer in the firm of Boulton and Watt, made the first self-moving engine in England. It is said that he made a small model and, after trying it out in his room, took it at dusk into a quiet lane, where its sparks and snorting so frightened a passing clergyman that he thought it was the Devil!

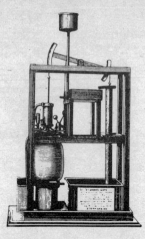

An Early Steam
Engine

For some reason, Murdoch gave up his experiments, but he told their secrets to young *Richard Trevithick*, who made a model engine so successfully that he took it to London and put it in a show.

Trevithick's Circular Railroad on Show in Euston Square, London, in 1809

Then Trevithick built the world's first railway engine, which pulled ten tons of iron along one of the early rail tracks in South Wales. Two difficulties arose: the rails kept breaking and the workers refused to let his engine run, because they were afraid that the men who looked after the horses would soon be out of work.

Discouraged, Trevithick went off to South America to try to make his fortune.

Blenkinsop's Rack Locomotive (1812)

The next engine was built at Leeds and was called *Blenkinsop's Rack Locomotive*, because it had a gear wheel which fitted into the teeth of a rack laid alongside the rails. But this idea did not last in England, and in 1813, *Hedley's Puffing Billy* and its sister *Wylam Dilly* were built without this device. They ran successfully up and down the line at Wylam Colliery, near Newcastle, pulling trucks of coal.

Puffing Billy

THE FIRST PUBLIC RAILWAY

It was at Wylam that *George Stephenson* was born. He was the son of a poor man and he did not go to school. He had to wait until he was eighteen before he could pay for lessons in reading and writing. Stephenson became an engineer, and when he heard about *Puffing Billy* he went over to Wylam, his old home, to see it for himself.

The Rocket

The Opening of the Stockton and Darlington Railway in 1825

Presently he persuaded his employer, the owner of the coalmine where he worked, to let him build a locomotive. He constructed one similar to *Puffing Billy* and called it *Blucher*, after the Prussian general who was at Waterloo with Wellington.

Stephenson now began his great work of building locomotives. Parliament, after a great deal of argument, gave permission for him to build a railway line between Stockton and Darlington. This line, the first public railway line, was opened in 1825. Its first train, pulled by Stephenson's engine called *Locomotion*, travelling at the great speed of twelve miles per hour, was made up of twelve trucks of coal and twenty-one waggons filled with passengers.

THE RAINHILL TRIALS

After this triumph came the famous Rainhill Trials. A railway line from Manchester to Liverpool was planned, and Stephenson was put in charge of the difficult task of laying the line, part of which ran over swampy land. It took him three years to finish the track, and then the owners were uncertain whether the waggons should be pulled along by horses, by cable or by locomotives. Eventually they offered a prize of £500 for the best engine. The trials were held at Rainhill in 1829, and the engines made ten trips up and down a stretch of line 1¾ miles long. Four engines entered the competition: the *Novelty*, the *Perseverance*, the *Sans Pareil* and the *Rocket*, which was built by George Stephenson and his son Robert. Reaching a speed of twenty-nine miles per hour, the *Rocket* easily won the prize and brought fame to the Stephensons.

THE RAILWAY CRAZE

After the Rainhill Trials nothing could stop the spread of railways. People tumbled over each other in their eagerness to subscribe money towards the opening of new railway lines to Birmingham, to Bristol, to Leeds and to every town of any size and importance. These lines were rapidly built by gangs of labourers, or navvies.

There were, of course, people who objected to the railways. Some landowners refused to allow the lines to run through their estates, which is one of the reasons

why certain towns today have their railway stations some distance away. But despite many difficulties the railways spread rapidly, and only fifteen years after the *Rocket's* triumph, people were travelling in trains all over the country. The stage-coach companies were ruined, and the last run of the mail-coach was drawing near.

TRAVELLING ON THE NEW RAILWAYS

Travel by the old stage-coaches had never been very comfortable, especially for the outside passengers, and the new railway carriages were no great improvement.

First-class carriages had cushioned seats, but the roofs were low and the windows small, so that they were stuffy in summer and cold in winter, since no heating was provided.

The second-class carriages had wooden benches, and the third-class carriages had no seats and no roof. They were just open trucks, and it is easy to imagine how miserable a journey could be on a wet, cold day.

Although travel by rail was uncomfortable, the journey was far quicker and cheaper than by stagecoach. This was partly because Parliament insisted that the railways must carry third-class passengers at a penny a mile. Ordinary people could travel to places which their fathers had never seen.

At first there were no signal-boxes. The driver simply kept a look-out for anything on the line and the passengers hoped his brakes were good. The first signalmen, called railway policemen, used flags and lamps, while signals were round or square boards on poles.

Below left: Model of a Signal used in 1837. The ball was lowered to the ground for "danger" or hoisted to the top to indicate "all clear". A lamp was used at night.

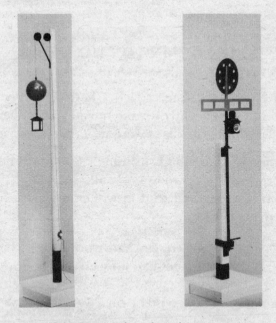

Above right: Model of a Signal used on the G.W.R. in 1841. When the crossbar and red light faced the driver, the signal was at "danger." For "line clear," the signal was turned sideways and the round disc faced the driver.

GAUGES

Stephenson built his railways with a width, or gauge, of 4 feet 8½ inches (1.435 metres), which is now the standard gauge of our railways. As more and more railways were built, it became clear that their rails should be the same distance apart, or it would be impossible for rolling-stock to pass from one line to another.

The famous engineer, Brunel, chose a gauge of seven feet (2.1 metres) for the Great Western Railway, which he claimed would give smoother running and greater speeds. This gauge proved a nuisance, and in the end, the Great Western had to change to Stephenson's standard gauge.

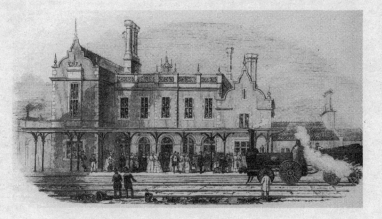

THE FIRST UNDERGROUND RAILWAY

Thousands of passengers came to London by train and added their numbers to the streets, already overcrowded with horse-omnibuses, hansom cabs, carriages and waggons. Some people suggested that the traffic problem would be helped by building overhead or underground railways. Finally, despite many jokes about such an idea, it was decided to run trains in tunnels under the ground.

The Opening of the
Metropolitan Railway

The Metropolitan Railway, opened in 1863, was the first of its kind. It was not very far below ground because chimneys and vents had to be made to let out the smoke from steam engines. By 1890 engineers had discovered how to run trains driven by electric motors, and gradually the London Underground grew to its present size. It is now the largest underground railway in the world.

City and South London
Railway, 1890—the First
Electric Tube Railway in
the World

9. TOWN TRAFFIC

A Brougham

STEAM-COACHES

In the towns the horse remained as important as ever for more than half a century. Steam-coaches in the streets had started to carry passengers as early as the railways, but in 1862 Parliament made a law that a horseless carriage must not travel faster than two miles per hour in the town, and a man with a red flag must walk ahead of it. With this law steam-coaches disappeared from the roads, and town traffic was again all horse-drawn.

A Victoria

THE HANSOM CAB

Sedan chairs had almost vanished from the London streets before Victoria came to the throne, and soon the heavy hackney-coaches were ousted by the hansom cab, named after its inventor, *Joseph Hansom*.

Hansom Cab 1842

Its neat appearance, with the cabby up behind, made it one of the everyday sights of London throughout Victoria's reign and until well into the twentieth century.

Hackney Coach 1842

HORSE-DRAWN BUSES

The Victorian horse-omnibuses were painted red, green, blue, chocolate, yellow and white, according to their route, so that passengers looked for the colour of their bus, not for its number.

To get as many passengers as possible, the drivers of the rival omnibus companies raced at top speed between bus-stops, where the conductors leapt down and snatched passers-by on board, or fought their rivals for the waiting passengers !

The early horse-bus carried its passengers inside, and there were a couple of seats on the box, next to the driver. So many people came to London for the Great Exhibition of 1851 that the omnibus companies took the daring step of putting passengers on the roof.

Those who travelled on the roof sat back-to-back on long forms. Only men went 'on top' since ladies in their long, trailing skirts could not be expected to climb the iron ladder.

Inside a Horse-Bus

BICYCLES

In 1868, over fifty years after the *dandy-horse*, came the *boneshaker*, with its wooden wheels and iron tyres. It had pedals and so was the forerunner of the modern bicycle. There was no chain, and the pedals were fixed to the front wheel. When going downhill they whizzed round so fast that the rider had to take his feet off.

Next came the *ordinary*, usually known as the *penny-farthing*, with its huge front wheel and at the back a little one, only about 35 centimetres across. The pedals were fixed to the front hub, so, by one turn of the pedals, the big wheel carried the rider forward a considerable distance.

The
Boneshaker

He sat perched up, 1½ metres in the air, and pedalled furiously along the roads in a cloud of dust. Riding a *penny-farthing* was hard, and even dangerous work. It was not long before steel, instead of wood, was used for bicycles, and solid rubber tyres were fitted. Even so, only the most daring of ladies would mount a bicycle. Tricycles were considered much safer.

A *Penny-Farthing*

The first bicycle to resemble those that we ride nowadays was *Mr. Stanley's safety bicycle,* a Rover, made at Coventry in 1885. The wheels were of equal size, and its pedals drove it along by means of a chain connected to the back hub. Three years later came *Dunlop's* pneumatic, or air-filled tyres, which made riding much more comfortable.

Rover Bicycle
1885

With the arrival of the *safety bicycle* many ladies took up cycling. It would have been impossible, however, to cycle in the long, flowing skirts which were fashionable, so a special cycling outfit was invented, called the Rational Costume. Lady cyclists wore a man's Norfolk jacket, a trilby hat, woollen stockings and knickerbockers.

10. SHIPS

THE STEAMSHIP

While Trevithick, Hedley and Stephenson were using steam-power to drive locomotives, other engineers were trying to use this same power in ships. As already mentioned on page 34. Symington's *Charlotte Dundas* and Bell's little *Comet* were in use before Waterloo. By 1815 steamers appeared on the river Thames and were making cross-Channel trips.

A Steam Vessel
of About
1812

In 1825 the General Steam Navigation Company, the oldest ocean-going steamship company in the world, had fifteen steamers, some of only 240 tons with two 40 h.p. engines, engaged on trade between London and the ports of Europe.

The *Neptune* 1842
(General Steam Navigation Co.)

The little wooden *Savannah* of 300 tons was the first
steamship to cross the Atlantic (1818). During the next
twenty years, regular crossings were made, and were
much faster than voyages by sailing ship. The paddle-
steamers *Sirius* and *Great Western* made the crossing in
nineteen days (1838), while sailing ships usually took
about thirty-three days.

The *William Fawcett* 1837
(P. & O. Line)

The famous P. & O. Line (Peninsular and Orient) started with the little *William Fawcett*, which sailed from Falmouth to Gibraltar in 1837, and soon, other P. & O. ships were making trips to India and the East.

Three years later *Samuel Cunard* founder of the famous Cunard Line, which has ever since rivalled the White Star Company on the Atlantic crossing. His ship *Britannia*, a vessel of over 1,000 tons, had engines of 740 h.p. and sailed at ten knots. (A knot is a speed of one sea mile an hour, or 1.15 miles.) She crossed the Atlantic in 14 days.

The *Britannia* 1840

People scoffed at the idea of building ships of iron instead of oak until an iron ship, the *Great Britain*, built to *Brunel's* plans, crossed the Atlantic in fifteen days. About a year later she went aground on the Irish coast, but she was saved, because she was made of iron. A wooden ship would have been broken up by the waves.

The arrival of iron ships meant that larger vessels could be built, though no one dreamed of liners so vast as the *Queen Mary* and *Queen Elizabeth*, which are both over 80,000 tons.

Here we must mention the *Great Eastern*, for she was the wonder and the failure of her age. When Brunel designed this ship, the biggest ship in the world was about 3,400 tons. He planned to make the *Great Eastern* 18,000 tons.

I. K. Brunel, the Great Engineer
(An early photograph)

This vast ship was designed to carry four thousand passengers and a large cargo, as well as the coal needed to drive the engines. For long voyages, sailing ships were still an advantage, since they did not have to carry coal. All available space was used for cargo.

The *Great Eastern* had paddles, and also a screw, but this idea did not work, because a screw could not function properly in water churned up by the paddles. She had five funnels and six masts, and she was so big that she had to be launched sideways into the Thames at Millwall. Unfortunately she stuck fast for several months and her owners went bankrupt.

The *Great Eastern*

She was sold and put on the Atlantic crossing instead of the long Australian route for which she was designed. Her speed was 14 knots, but her great size could not be fully used in those days, and she did not pay her expenses.

In 1865-66 she helped to lay the telegraph cables across the Atlantic, but after that useful job was finished, poor *Great Eastern* was just a curiosity. For a time she was used as a floating fair, but finally she was broken up for scrap iron.

Despite the failure of the *Great Eastern*, the steamship had come to stay, but there was still a glorious spell of life ahead for sailing-ships. On very long voyages, such as those from India, China and Australia, round the

Cape of Good Hope, the sailing ships were not only more useful, but actually faster, especially for such cargoes as tea and wool, which needed to reach their markets quickly

THE CLIPPERS

The clipper ships, sometimes called windjammers, were specially built for fast sailing to China and Australia. The Americans led the way at first with better ships than ours, but British firms began to build equally well. Many a famous race took place when tea and wood clippers beat up the Channel, carrying every possible yard of canvas, in the effort to win the prize offered by merchants for the first ship to dock at London.

The *Cutty Sark*

The clippers were wonderful ships and masterpieces of craftmanship. They were faster than almost any steamer afloat, being capable of 17 knots. Of all these graceful ships, perhaps the most famous was the *Cutty Sark*, built as a tea-clipper and afterwards used on the Australian wool run.

Eventually steamships defeated the clippers, for the opening of the Suez Canal provided a shorter route to the East. This route was useless to sailing ships, as they would be becalmed on the canal for lack of wind.

By 1890 the day of the clippers was almost over and only a few continued to make the long trip from Australia.

Two Famous Clippers, *Ariel* and *Taeping;* racing up-Channel

MODERN SHIPS

Meanwhile steamships improved. The Cunard Line built the *Servia* of steel instead of iron, and other

R.M.S. *Servia* 1881

companies followed this example. Then came a new form of engine, the steam-turbine, which gave ships speeds of from 20 to 30 knots.

Probably the ship with the proudest record was the first *Mauretania* (1907) 31,900 tons. She held the Atlantic crossing record, known as the Blue Riband, for over

The *Mauretania*

twenty years, from 1907 until 1929. In more recent times others have taken her place: the German liner *Bremen*, the great French *Normandie*, our own *Queen Mary* and *Queen Elizabeth*, the *United States* and the *Canberra*.

The *Queen Elizabeth*

11. THE ROYAL NAVY

Throughout Victoria's reign the Royal Navy slowly changed from sail to steam, from wood to iron and from iron to steel. Muzzle-loading guns were replaced by breech loaders, round cannon balls by conical shot and the old broadside guns by turrets.

H.M.S. *Dreadnought*
1914

Early in the twentieth century came the first of the modern warships, the *Dreadnought*, with armour-plate, explosive shells, wireless and torpedoes. There followed the host of ships, big and small, which make up a modern navy, destroyers, submarines, cruisers and aircraft-carriers.

The bad old custom of forcing seamen into service by the Press Gang came to an end in 1853. From this time forward, men could sign on for an honourable career in the Royal Navy. It is interesting to know that a regular uniform for naval seamen did not come into use until 1857.

The Battleship
H.M.S. *Howe*
1942

12. WARS IN QUEEN VICTORIA'S REIGN

Since William IV's reign our soldiers had worn red coats, with white or blue trousers and a tall cap called a shako, though the Guards wore bearskins. The cavalry, known as dragoons and hussars, wore even handsomer uniforms and were armed with lances, sabres and long pistols, called carbines.

French and English Fleets bombard Sevastopol during the Crimean War

The wars in Queen Victoria's reign were fought far from this country, and disturbed little, if at all, the life of the ordinary citizen.

The Crimean War, in which Florence Nightingale won fame, was fought against Russia on the shores of the Black Sea. *The Indian Mutiny* caused the British Government to take over the rule of India from the East India Company.

Foot Soldiers of The Crimean War

In these wars foot-soldiers were armed with the rifle, which was still muzzle-loaded. The soldier bit off the end of a paper cartridge, poured the gunpowder down the barrel, and rammed home the wad and the bullet. For charges and all close work the bayonet was fixed to the rifle and used like a lance.

Officer of the Dragoon Guards
Crimean War

Cannons were now known as field-guns or artillery. They fired grape shot against troops, and cannon balls against forts and buildings. These tore holes in the walls, but did not explode like modern shells.

A Mounted Soldier of the Indian
Mutiny

In *The Boer War*, against the Dutch settlers in South Africa, rifles, which were loaded at the breech instead of at the muzzle, were introduced. The barrel was grooved, causing the bullet to spin as it passed through. This made shooting more accurate than firing through a plain tube. The first machine-guns, called Gatlings, were also in use at this time.

Explosive shells, balloons, searchlights and despatch-riders on bicycles were introduced. This was the last war in which cavalry was widely used with success.

Khaki, which was already in use in India, became the colour of uniforms in war-time, for in a dry and dusty country it made our soldiers more difficult to see. The splendid uniforms of scarlet and gold, with gleaming helmets and plumes, are now reserved for special occasions in peace-time.

The simple warfare when two armies formed up and marched towards each other in broad daylight and fought, while the generals watched the battle from a short distance away, had vanished.

Soldiers—Boer War

Modern warfare was coming, with all its terrible weapons, aimed not only at soldiers and sailors, but against ordinary men, women and children.

13. THE POST

In Tudor times royal messengers and the servants of great men carried letters and despatches for their masters to all parts of the kingdom. Charles I and the Stuarts allowed people to use the royal service of post-horses if they paid a fee when the letter was delivered. The letters were merely folded and sealed with a blob of wax. Even as early as 1660 post-dates were stamped on letters.

William Dockwra started a private Penny Post in London in 1680. It was so successful that it was very soon taken over as part of the royal service, and the fees for letters made up a useful part of the King's income.

By Georgian days the post-boys who carried the mails proved lazy and dishonest. They were replaced by the famous mail-coaches, which ran on regular routes to and from Lombard Street in London, with the mail-

One of the popular sights in the early nineteenth century was the departure of the mail-coaches each evening from the General Post Office.

bags in the charge of the guard. The cost of sending a letter depended on the distance it had to travel. As the fee was often high, people began to dodge payment by giving letters and messages to the coachmen to deliver privately.

Rowland Hill discovered a satisfactory way out of this difficulty. In 1840 he started the Penny Post. A letter cost a penny for each half ounce, no matter how far it had to travel.

The letter was paid for when posted, instead of on arrival, and this led to the use of postage stamps and envelopes. The first British stamp bore the head of the young Queen Victoria, and was called the Penny Black.

TELEGRAMS

Telegraphy, the method of passing messages along an electrified wire, was invented by an Englishman named *Wheatstone* and improved by *Samuel Morse* in America. The first telegraph service was installed in 1838 on the London and Blackwall Railway. As the railways spread all over England, telegraph poles were erected alongside the tracks.

Messages could now be sent in a few minutes to distant places, whereas, not so very long before, it had taken a messenger on horseback several days to reach them. Today we have become so used to the idea of speed that it is difficult to realise how very wonderful this invention seemed to the Victorians.

THE TELEPHONE

Somewhat later, in 1876, telephones were invented by *Alexander Graham Bell*, a Scotsman who settled in Boston, America. At first they were expensive and people were slow to have these strange instruments installed. By 1900 only 10,000 were in use in this country. The Electric Telegraph Company and the National Telephone Company, which operated these useful services in their early days, were eventually taken over by the Post Office.

A Telephone of 1900

Alexander Graham Bell's First Telephone

14. POOR PEOPLE
IN VICTORIAN DAYS

CHILDREN AT WORK

In the first half of Queen Victoria's long reign there were a great many poor people in London and the big factory towns. Hordes of ragged, dirty children were to be seen in the streets, earning a living as best they could. Little boys and girls, hoping for a halfpenny, would rush to sweep the road clean for any lady or gentleman wishing to cross the muddy highway, and others would hold bridles of waiting horses for a penny.

By the Thames, lads called 'mudlarks' waded at low tide in the filthy mud, searching for scraps of iron and lead to sell.

Hundreds of these ragged urchins had never been to school or had a good meal in their lives. They spent their days picking and stealing, to make a few pence to take home to their families living in tumbledown houses and miserable alleys.

A Mudlark

There were many children who had no homes at all. They slept among barrows in the great markets or under railway bridges. They begged for food or searched dustbins for scraps to eat.

In the factory towns at this time, children of six and seven years worked at the machines from early in the morning until evening, for a few pence each week. The hours were so long that many fell asleep from weariness. Their mothers worked twelve and fourteen hours a day, too, yet there was seldom enough to eat at home, and certainly little warmth or clothing.

Orphans from the Workhouse were housed by the factory owner in the 'prentice house, where they slept in shifts. This means that one set of children were in bed while another set were working. They spent nearly all their waking hours at work. There was no holiday on Saturday and part of Sunday was spent on cleaning the machines.

Women and children worked down the coal-mines. They pushed the coal-trucks, or sat for hours in the darkness working the ventilation doors, or crawled along on all fours like animals, harnessed to a truck with a chain.

Boys at Work in a Mine

Women Carrying Coal

All this unhappiness and poverty puzzled kindly people when they learned about it from a book published in 1842. But even so, many of them thought that such things could not be avoided and were even necessary. "The poor," they said, "are ever with us."

STREET LIFE

A man called *Henry Mayhew* went into the poorest parts of London to find out for himself how the people lived, and afterwards he wrote a book about all he had seen.

A London Slum

He discovered that the poorest people of all lived in slums called 'rookeries,' which were clusters of tumbledown, ancient houses built round filthy courts and alleys. The people who lived there, workmen, pedlars, beggars and thieves, had many odd ways of making their living.

First, there were the costermongers, who sold fruit, vegetables and other things from their donkey-barrows.

They were rough, lively men, dressed in corduroys with pearly buttons. They were fond of gambling, singing, and fighting, but they were kind to their bulldogs and donkeys.

"Cats' and Dogs' Meat"

Then there were hordes of street-sellers, who cried out
their wares in the streets:

     sellers of fly-papers
     walking-sticks and whips
     pipes, snuff and tobacco boxes
     old clothes

All these and many other odd things were sold all day
long:

     needles and spoons
     boiled puddings
     cakes, tarts, gingerbread
     hot green peas
     dogs' meat
     pea-soup and hot eels
     live animals and birds
     watercress

Street Bird Seller

Jack Black
Her Majesty's Ratcatcher

Other less respectable tradesmen were: old-clothes
men, rabbit-skin buyers, rag-pickers, and sewer-
hunters, who entered the London sewers at low tide
and searched the ancient, dangerous tunnels for
anything of value.

Long-Song Seller

Flower Girl

London Costermonger

Dustman

There were dog-stealers who carried a bag into which they popped any good-looking dog. Later on, they claimed a reward from the owner, for 'finding' it.

Some of the cries were:
"Fresh watercresses!"
"Ha'penny, half-pint, Milk. O!"
"Here's all hot! Here's all hot!" (pies)
"Catch 'em alive, only a ha'penny!" (flypapers)
"Oysters, penny a lot!"

There were also large numbers of wandering workmen who called at respectable houses or shouted their trade in every street. There were scissors-grinders, chair-menders, mat-menders, rat-catchers, shoe-blacks and chimney-sweeps. Every chimney-sweep had his boy who, brush in hand, was forced to climb up inside the chimneys.

London Coffee Stall

At this time, less than one hundred years ago, when Dickens was living in London and writing his books, street-musicians were to be seen and heard every day. There was the German band, the Italian hurdy-gurdy man with his monkey in a little red cap, the barrel-organ grinder, the ballad singer and the one-man band, in which one man played several instruments at the same time. He had pan-pipes in his mouth, a drum on his back, which he beat with a stick tied to his elbow, cymbals on top of the drum, clashed by means of a string tied to one heel, and a triangle in his hand!

There were jugglers, Punch and Judy Shows, stilt walkers, performing dogs and dancing bears. Lastly, those with nothing to sell and no tricks to perform begged for a living.

Street Musicians in Leicester Square

Foreigners who came to London, the richest city in the world in those days, were horrified at the large number of beggars in every street and thoroughfare.

There were two more entertainments to be seen any day in the London streets: the evening newspaper boy on his penny-farthing bicycle, scorching through the traffic and between the horse-buses at breakneck speed, and the fire-engine, drawn by two galloping grey horses, clearing its way, not by a bell, but by the yelling of its entire crew.

LORD SHAFTESBURY

Lord Shaftesbury was the leader of a group of men and women who were ashamed that children were forced to work long hours in factories and coal mines.

When he tried to persuade Parliament to forbid children working more than ten hours a day, he was told that such a law would ruin the country and the cotton-trade of Lancashire!

But he refused to give in, and at last Parliament agreed that children under thirteen years must not work more than eight hours a day, and women and children must no longer be sent underground to work in the mines. Rules were made for factories, and inspectors were sent round to see that they were obeyed.

It was some time before very much notice was taken of the new laws, but gradually throughout Queen Victoria's reign working conditions improved, especially for poor children.

Following Lord Shaftesbury's example, many clergymen, preachers and ladies from well-to-do families, of whom Florence Nightingale is the most famous, began to help the poor.

These splendid men and women spent their lives trying to improve a world which had grown hard and cruel.

Florence Nightingale Nursing Wounded Soldiers at the Crimean War

Eaton Hall, Cheshire, a Large House in the 'new-Gothic' style

15. THE VICTORIANS

HOUSES

The builders of Queen Anne's reign and of Georgian days knew how to build a house which was handsome and pleasing in proportion. During Victorian days there were great changes in style, and houses became ugly in shape and grossly overdecorated. Perhaps in the haste to make money there was no time for beauty and good taste in buildings, furniture and pictures, or perhaps the people who could not see the misery of the poor, and the ugliness of the factory towns, were just as blind to fair and shapely things.

If a picture, a chair or a house is badly shaped, it cannot be improved afterwards by putting on a lot of fancy and unnecessary decoration. Yet this is exactly what many Victorian builders tried to do. Their houses were ugly in shape, and every kind of pinnacle, turret, balcony and iron railing was added.

A Room in Osborne House, Queen Victoria's Mansion on the Isle of Wight

Another popular fashion of the time was the building of imitation castles and vast hideous country houses in the Gothic style of churches and cathedrals of the later Middle Ages. The 'new-Gothic' style was an imitation of the glorious arches and spires of the Middle Ages, and quite unsuitable for houses.

A Victorian House

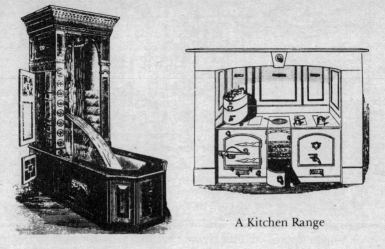

A Kitchen Range

A New Bath

Although there were many curious houses built at this time, not all Victorian houses were like this. And even though their outside appearance may have been unpleasing, inside they were beginning to include conveniences such as bathrooms, lavatories and hot water systems, which in former days had existed only in a very few homes of the rich. It was, however, many years before bathrooms were common. Most people used a washstand in their bedroom.

Gas-lighting indoors became general, and has only recently been widely replaced by electricity. Gas cookers were on show in the 1851 exhibition, but most Victorian houses were fitted with the kitchen range, which had, taken the place of the open fire. In its day the range was a great advance on any other stove. There was the fire in the centre and an oven on one side, heated by hot air, and a water tank on the other, with a tap from which hot water could be drawn off.

Brass Bedstead

FURNITURE

Much of the Victorian furniture suffered from the same faults as the houses. The grace of Heppelwhite and Chippendale furniture was replaced by fussy furniture with far too much ornament, and it was usually made of mahogany, brass or iron.

People with plenty of money often had homes crowded with furniture. Never were rooms so cluttered up with chairs, tables, occasional tables, plant pot stands, overmantels, pianos, bookcases, fretwork and strange pieces called 'whatnots.'

Fireplace

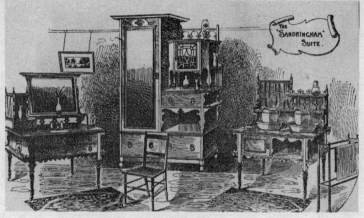

Bedroom Furniture, including a Wash-stand

Windows were heavily draped with lace curtains and inner curtains of heavy material. Tables were covered with cloths with fringes and bobbles round the edges and even the piano legs were given frills.

Sideboard

Huge pictures in velvet frames and dark photographs of the whole family covered the walls, while shelves and china cabinets were laden with vases, plants and wax fruit under glass cases.

CLOTHES IN VICTORIAN DAYS

At the beginning of Victoria's reign ladies wore a great many clothes: five or six petticoats under dresses of silk and taffeta. Waists were so tiny that ladies often fainted because their corsets were laced too tightly!

Poke bonnets and shawls were fashionable. Dresses for dance or ball were low-cut, leaving the shoulders bare.

Men's clothes became quieter in colour, and a neck-cloth tied in a knot was worn instead of our collars and ties.

In the middle of the reign came the crinoline, a full hooped petticoat, which expanded the skirt worn over it.

Next came the bustle, a pad or cushion worn at the back, just below the waist line, to make a lady's skirt stand out behind.

Later, dresses with leg-of-mutton sleeves were fashionable, and muffs and fans reappeared.

Almost every Victorian gentleman wore a beard or moustache, though some preferred side-whiskers called mutton-chops and Dundrearies. Beards came back into fashion during the Crimean War, in imitation of the soldiers.

Cigarettes also appeared at this time, for the soldiers copied this manner of smoking from the Turkish troops.

Towards the end of Victoria's reign men's clothes became more and more like our present-day style, except that trousers were tighter and top-hats and bowler hats were worn by everybody.

Quite humble clerks went to the office every morning in a topper, and only costers and cads at the Derby wore caps.

Straw boaters, both for ladies and gentlemen, were fashionable in the summer.

Here is a family at the end of Queen Victoria's reign.

A Dame School

SCHOOLS

For many years schools of various kinds had existed, but there were very few for children of poor parents.

The great Public Schools such as Eton, Harrow and Rugby had become expensive schools for children of the well-to-do. There were also the old Grammar Schools, many of them dating back to the time of Edward VI and Elizabeth. To these went the sons of merchants and citizens who were able to pay the fees.

Many children of wealthy parents did not go to school at all but were taught by a governess or tutor in the schoolrooms of their big houses.

Girls' schools were few in number. They taught deportment (how to walk and sit gracefully), manners, needlework, dancing and a little music and reading. For the most part, girls were expected to learn at home how to run a house, how to cook and how to make preserves and jams, wines, and simple medicines.

Lastly, there were Dame Schools, where an old lady taught a few village children in her cottage. Local people gave a small sum of money for this work.

There were also many children who worked in factories and had no time for schooling. Christian men and women were distressed that these boys and girls were growing up ignorant of Jesus Christ and unable to read and write. They started Sunday Schools and Church Day Schools. Sometimes children already at work came to school for part of the day. By the time Victoria became queen the Government had begun to help these good people to build schools.

As a result of Lord Shaftesbury's Factory Acts, children now had time for school. In 1870 Parliament insisted that every child must go to school from the age of five until thirteen, and that parents must pay a little — about sixpence ($2\frac{1}{2}$p) — towards the cost.

Monitors Teaching Groups of Younger Boys

A London Schoolroom at the end of Victoria's Reign

Many schools were now built. These were called 'Board Schools,' because they were managed by a Board, or Committee, of Managers. Those built by the Churches were usually known as 'National Schools.' Nowadays these schools would be considered very dull places indeed. Classes of sixty or eighty children had one teacher, who was helped by a young pupil-teacher, apprenticed for five years, to learn teaching.

In some schools it was the custom for 'monitors,' older children, to teach the younger children in groups arranged round the walls of a large room. The monitors pointed to letters and words, and the children recited them aloud. The Schoolmaster sat at a high desk to keep order. He was very strict and often used the cane. Lessons were usually Scripture, reading, writing and arithmetic.

At first, parents were very angry that their children had to go to school instead of earning money, and when builders came to put up a school in the slums, they were chased away!

VICTORIAN FAMILY LIFE

During the reign of Queen Victoria there was much poverty and misery, but for ordinary middle-class families it was a time of happy family life. Their way of life and many of their ideas may seem strange to us and often rather hard, but the Victorians were contented, and they were satisfied with few pleasures.

Father, known as Papa, with his beard or side-whiskers, was the Head of the House, and everyone, especially the children, treated him with the greatest respect. His word was law for all the household: his wife, children and servants. He sat at the head of the table and carved the great joint of meat at dinner, and the youngsters were not supposed to talk unless spoken to by a grown-up.

Mama kept her large family in order, and used a penny cane, if necessary. With eight, ten, twelve or more children, she was a very busy mother, for there were no

A Victorian Family At Home

vacuum-cleaners, washing-machines or electrical gadgets in the house. Tinned goods and foods prepared in packets were unknown. Clothes were mostly made at home or at a dressmaker's in the town. After she was thirty, Mama was considered quite middle-aged and often took to wearing a little lace cap in the house.

At the end of each day Papa took family prayers, when everyone, including the servants, knelt down in the dining-room or study. He also led the family to church on Sunday morning and again in the evening, when they sat in the family pew.

Papa   Mama

Sunday was a very solemn day and as little work as possible was done. No shops were open and there were certainly no amusements. Everyone put on their best clothes, which were usually stiff and uncomfortable.

On Sunday afternoons the family often went for a walk, but no games with a ball or hoop were allowed. Even picture books were forbidden on Sundays; Sunday reading included the Bible and certain books about the saints and missionaries.

A Victorian Musical Evening

The nineteenth century was a time of emigration from our overcrowded island and it was common for younger sons of these large families to go overseas to find work and to make their homes in Canada, Australia and New Zealand. Many, especially the Scots and the Irish, went to America.

The adventures and discoveries of such men as *David Livingstone* and *H. M. Stanley*, and later *Cecil Rhodes*, fired the imaginations of young men at home, and they set off to make their fortunes. Cargoes of cheap grain and meat coming from new lands across the sea ruined many of our own farmers, and this caused hundreds of farm workers to try their luck in one of the colonies, which we now call the Dominions.

Although there were no wireless sets, television, cinemas or motor-cars, the Victorians did not find life dull.

People worked longer hours, often twelve or fourteen hours a day. Shops opened before breakfast and stayed open until 9 o'clock at night and 11 p.m. on Saturdays. Half-days and annual holidays were rare.

Amusements were simple and the family often gathered round the piano to sing the latest popular songs, or they entertained each other by reciting or playing the piano. Public readings from Dickens, and recitations, were popular, and drew large audiences. In London and the large towns the music-halls were not considered quite respectable, but the theatre was sometimes visited. Children very rarely went to any entertainment, except perhaps to the circus or to a pantomime.

They had their parties, with many of the games which we still play today: hunt the slipper, postman's knock, blind man's bluff. Comics and magazines were not so common in those days. The best known were *The Boys' Own Paper, The Girls' Own Paper* and *Little Folks*.

Tennis in 1878
Reproduced by permission of the Proprietors of PUNCH

Playing Croquet

Books they had in plenty, but the pictures and covers were often dull. Many of the best children's stories were written in Victorian days: *Alice in Wonderland, The Water Babies, Tom Brown's Schooldays, Black Beauty, Little Women* and *Treasure Island.*

There were books of adventure by *R. M. Ballantyne; Jules Verne; G. A. Henty* and *Captain Marryat.* One of the most popular authors was *Charles Dickens*, whose books were read aloud to the eagerly assembled family.

Games had mysterious 'seasons': hoops, tops, marbles, hop-scotch came in and went out at their proper times. Battledore and shuttlecock, and an amusing game called diabolo, were fashionable. Grown-ups as well as children played croquet, a game in which the ladies' long skirts were less of a nuisance than at tennis.

At cricket the first Test Match was played in 1882, and the Football League was formed six years later, when it was common for footballers to play with caps on.

Toys were not so varied and splendid as they are to-day. It was the time of the rocking-horse and Noah's ark, of the wax-faced doll and boxes of tin and lead soldiers.

Magic lanterns, which threw pictures on to a screen, were a great novelty, and so were the model steam-engines with real boilers which were heated by methylated spirit.

At the end of the old Queen's long reign, and when your grandparents were young, Britain was the richest country on earth. Her ships sailed to the corners of the world, taking goods from her factories and bringing back gold, corn, frozen meat and every kind of food and luxury for rich and poor.

Battledore and Shuttlecock

Britain controlled most of the world's trade and ruled the biggest Empire ever known. People believed that she would grow even richer and greater, and that poverty and distress would finally disappear.

In 1901 the Queen died, after a reign of sixty-three years. Jovial Edward VII became king and everyone looked forward to peace and plenty.

The Old Queen

PART THREE
THE TWENTIETH CENTURY

Edward VII (1901-1910)

George V (1910-1936)

Edward VIII (1936)

George VI (1936-1952)

Elizabeth II (1952-　　)
Photograph by Dorothy Wilding

SOME OF THE CHIEF EVENTS

1901—A 1,000-mile race for motor-cars showed how this new invention was progressing.

1903—The first real film was made: 'The Great Train Robbery.'
The *Wright* brothers in America made the first aeroplane flight.

1909—*Bleriot* flew the English Channel.

1912—*Captain Scott's* Antarctic Expedition.

THE FIRST WORLD WAR

1914-1918 The Great War was fought by Britain, France and Russia, against Germany.
The war began with the invasion of Belgium and, by 1915, both great armies faced each other in trenches across Belgium and Northern France. Each side suffered greatly; Russia collapsed in 1917, but America entered the war and Germany was defeated in 1918. *Field Marshal Haig* commanded the British Forces for most of the war. *Lloyd George* was Prime Minister towards the end of the war.

1919—The League of Nations was set up at Geneva, Switzerland, where, it was hoped, nations would settle their quarrels instead of going to war.

1922—Broadcasting started from Marconi House.

1926—*Baird* demonstrated television.

1927—'Talkie' films arrived from America.

1935—*King George V's* Jubilee.

1936—The *Queen Mary* (81,000 tons) made her first voyage.

Television programmes relayed from Alexandra Palace.

THE SECOND WORLD WAR

1939-1945 The Second World War between *Hitler's* Nazi Germany, and Britain and France. The actual cause was the German attack on Poland, but, as before, the real cause was Germany's desire for power and more territory.

In 1940 the German armies conquered France and nearly all Europe. Italy, under the leadership of *Mussolini*, joined Hitler, but Britain, led by the Prime Minister, *Winston Churchill*, fought on alone.

The Battle of Britain, fought in the air, narrowly saved us from invasion. Hitler invaded Russia, and Japan attacked British and American possessions in the Far East.

In 1944, after many disasters, Britain and America invaded Normandy, and, following great Russian victories, the Allies defeated Germany by May 1945. Japan surrendered a few months later, after the Americans had dropped the first atomic bomb.

AFTER THE WAR

1946—The first meeting of the United Nations Organisation.

1947—The Indian Empire came to an end. Although India is now a republic, she is also a member of the Commonwealth and she acknowledges the Queen as head of the Commonwealth. Pakistan became a Dominion.

1950—War broke out in Korea and the first United Nations Army took the field.

1951—The Festival of Britain at South Bank, London.

1952—Accession of *Queen Elizabeth II*.

1953—Everest climbed by Hillary and Tensing.

1956—Suez Canal taken by President Nasser of Egypt.

1957—Ghana became a self-governing Dominion.

1958—Fuchs crossed the Antarctic via the South Pole.

1960—Nigeria granted independence.

1961—South Africa left the Commonwealth.

16. MOTOR-CARS

In the twentieth century two terrible World Wars have entirely changed the position of Britain, and she is no longer the richest and most powerful country in the world. But it is not only war which changes people's way of life.

In the last fifty years there have been inventions and discovereis, such as the motor-car and television, which have changed the everyday lives of ordinary people more than the Victorians would have believed possible. Although motor-cars were invented in Queen Victoria's reign, most people think of the twentieth century as the motor-car age.

The 'Red Flag' law of 1862 drove steam-carriages off the roads, because a man had to walk in front of such vehicles carrying a red flag. This not only made people laugh, but caused horseless carriages to be so slow that they were useless.

In France and Germany there was no such law, so engineers were able to follow Cugnot's work on the steam-coach.

One of their problems was to find a way of building a vehicle which was lighter than a locomotive, whose great weight would have broken up the roads.

It is generally agreed that a German, named *Benz*, built the first petrol-driven car in 1885. This was really a tricycle with a motor at the back.

Benz Three-Wheel Motor-Car 1888

Two years later another German, *Gottlieb Daimler*, built the first Daimler motor-car. Both men had found that the advantage of petrol over steam was that the engine could be smaller and lighter.

Once these first cars had appeared, others developed rapidly, especially in France, where a firm called *Panhard and Levasser* obtained permission to make Daimlers. In 1892 an American, *Henry Ford*, built the first of his famous cars, which were afterwards known as 'tin lizzies.'

The Red Flag Act was still hindering progress in England, but when the first car was brought over from France about 1895, it caused much excitement, and British engineers quietly began to start making cars.

Public interest and enthusiasm among wealthy people became so great that Parliament was persuaded to abolish the Reg Flag Law in 1896. Cars were then allowed on the road, but there was a speed limit of 14 miles per hour.

To celebrate this freedom, fifty of the new cars, which look comical to us nowadays, set off to run from London to Brighton to show the public how reliable and safe cars really were. Alas, quite a number of them broke down on the way!

The first British-built car was the *Lanchester*. Soon afterwards Daimler cars were made at Coventry.

Daimler 1895

The earliest cars were two-seaters, with no roof and poor springs. The engine was under the seat, and owners had to carry large cans of petrol and spare tyres with them. Cars were expensive and the early motorists, who felt themselves adventurous pioneers, were usually well-to-do folk.

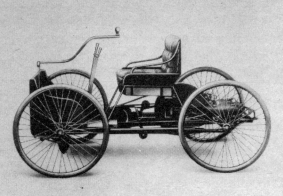

The First *Ford* Car

They wore goggles to protect their eyes from dust, and in winter, fur coats and thick boots. They took no notice of the rude remarks of pedestrians, but waved cheerily to every motorist they passed, and always stopped to assist a fellow-adventurer who was in trouble by the roadside.

Lanchester Motor-Car 1892

Motorists of 1905 in a *Swift*

By 1901 motor-cars had begun to take the shape which is familiar to us to-day. They were much higher, and they were roofless, but the engine was now in front of the driver, and there were windscreens, gear-boxes, rubber tyres and large brass lamps.

Members of the Royal Family out for a Drive

Model T *Ford* 1909

Such makes as *Humber, Riley, Lagonda, Sunbeam, Singer, Napier* and *Swift* were already on the road, and had advanced sufficiently to take part in a 1,000-mile race round Britain. The new king, Edward VII, was an enthusiastic supporter of motoring, which was looked upon as a sport.

New life came back to the roads, and they began to hum with traffic again. At first, however, cars frightened people. Their sudden explosions caused horses to bolt, and their rubber tyres sucked up dust from the roads in great white clouds.

Lady Motor-Cyclist

The roads would have rapidly broken up under this treatment, if it had not been discovered that spraying with tar not only solved the problem of dust, but gave smoother roads and fewer punctures.

Unlike aeroplanes, motor-cars did not make great strides during the 1914-18 War, probably because it was a war of trenches and not of movement.

Tank of 1918

The tank arrived late in the war, in an attempt to break through the enemy's deep defences. The first tanks looked like this and they gradually developed into the great *Shermans* and *Centurions* of today.

Centurion Tank

One of the last Horse-drawn Buses — the 2d. Bus over Waterloo
Bridge

After the Great War motor-cars advanced quickly.
Saloon bodies were built in the 1920s, and *Henry Ford*
led the way in producing large numbers of cheap cars
for people of moderate incomes. The Ford, Austin and
Morris works produced cars in huge factories, and at
one time a Ford saloon cost only £100. In 1904 there
were 8,000 private cars in the country, but in 1960 there
were over 5,250,000.

The First Trolley-Bus or Rail-less Tramcar

Buses and taxis gradually defeated the hansom cabs and horse-omnibuses, just as surely as lorries and vans have ousted carts and waggons, and tractors have almost entirely replaced farm-horses. By 1913 the horse-omnibus and horse-tramcar had gone from London streets, though the hansom cab lingered on.

Modern traffic has caused a problem far worse than in the days of quarrelsome hackney-coach drivers and waggoners, because the speed of traffic causes so many accidents and deaths. There was an outcry in 1908 when two people were knocked down in London,

Steam Omnibus racing Horse Buses in London

especially as the speed limit had been raised to 20 miles per hour. In 1930 over 7,000 people were killed on the roads, and over 6,000 in 1960. Although Belisha beacons, roundabouts and a 30 mile-per-hour limit in towns were introduced in the 1930's, no one has yet solved the problem of danger on the road, which is far worse than that of the highwayman, robbers and footpads of old times.

17. BALLOONS

The dream of flying through the air has fascinated men for hundreds of years. There were many men who thought they might be able to fly with wings on their arms like a bird, but this was an impossible dream.

A Montgolfier Hot-air Balloon

Men first succeeded in flying by means of balloons, lifted by hot air or hydrogen gas. The first aerial voyage was made in a hot-air balloon built by two Frenchmen, the *Montgolfier* brothers. It was piloted by *De Rozier* and *D'Arlandes* who flew for five miles over Paris on November 21st 1783, with a brazier of hot coals hung in the neck of the balloon to keep the air hot. A month later, a French scientist, *Monsieur Charles*, with a craftsman named *Robert*; made several flights in a balloon filled with hydrogen.

The Basket of a Modern Balloon

The first balloon voyage in England was made by *Lunardi*; an Italian, in 1784, when he took a cat and a pigeon with him from London. *Sadler*; an Oxford grocer, was the first Englishman to fly in this way. Next year, the Frenchman, *Blanchard*; and an American, *Dr. Jefferies*, made a perilous crossing of the Channel, during which they had to throw overboard most of their clothing, including Blanchard's trousers, to lessen the weight.

The English airship R 101

After this, balloons became very popular, and, by Napoleon's time, they were used for military spotting of the enemy. These were captive balloons, tethered by long ropes and filled with hydrogen or coal-gas.

The chief difficulty with balloons was to steer them. It was easy to go up by throwing ballast overboard, and to go down by letting out gas through a valve, but the direction in which the balloonists travelled depended upon the wind.

It was the French who first elongated balloons to make them into airships and fitted them with engines and rudders. The first one, using a steam engine, was flown in 1852, but it was too slow and clumsy to be successful.

Later, electric and petrol motors were used and, in 1900, a German, Count Zeppelin, built the first of the huge airships known as "zeppelins." These airships were used in 1910 for the first air service in the world, and travelled between Berlin and Switzerland.

Zeppelins were also used for the first bombing of London in the Great War of 1914-1918. Between 1931 and 1937 the famous *Graf Zeppelin* made regular passenger trips across the Atlantic at a speed of about 60 miles per hour.

British airships were also built, and one known as the *R34* made the first double crossing of the Atlantic. Larger and larger airships were made, but there were many disasters. After the loss of the *R101*, the bursting into flames of the *Hindenburg* over New York, and the destruction of two large American airships it was decided not to build further airships.

18. AEROPLANES

As with most inventions, aeroplanes took a long time to develop. An Englishman, *Sir George Cayley*, made the first model glider in 1804. Then for nearly a century there were many experiments, including several powered models and a few unsuccessful full-scale machines.

The First Aeroplane Flight, 1903

At the end of the century, a German, *Otto Lilienthal*, successfully flew full-sized gliders. In 1896 he crashed in one of these and was killed.

Two American brothers, *Wilbur* and *Orville Wright*, mastered gliding and then built and flew the first powered aeroplane in 1903, at Kitty Hawk in North Carolina. Within two years, they had made an aeroplane which could turn, circle and keep flying for half an hour.

Wilbur Wright taking his first woman passenger, 1908

Little progress was made in Europe until Wilbur
Wright came to France in 1908 and showed how an
aeroplane could be flown and controlled. At once,
flying became popular.

Mr. Grahame White, one of the English Aircraft Pioneers

When *Monsieur Blériot* flew across the Channel in 1909, his feat aroused enormous interest and enthusiasm.

The rest of the story is like the motor-car; larger, faster and more reliable machines, which have brought us to our present jet aircraft, flying faster than sound can travel. The farthest corners of the world are now nearer for the traveller than Exeter was to London in the days of the stagecoach.

A Blériot monoplane, about 1910

Aeroplanes were greatly developed during the Great War of 1914-18, for every big nation built up its Air Force of fighters, bombers and seaplanes, with all the speed and skill which war forces upon men's minds and hands.

After that war there were thousands of planes and pilots ready to turn to civil flying. The British, who had not made great progress in the air until the war, now produced some fine pilots to explore the routes over which passenger planes would soon make regular trips.

A Military Aeroplane about 1915

Alcock and *Brown*, in 1919, were the first men to fly the Atlantic; two brothers, *Ross* and *Keith Smith*, flew to Australia. *Alan Cobham* won fame by his flights to India, South Africa and Melbourne. These airmen were brave adventurers, for they flew over unknown routes without any help on the way from weather reports, landing grounds, air control or ground crews.

Sopwith *Camel* — famous Fighter Plane of the First World War (1917)

The Vickers *Vimy* in which Alcock and Brown made their great
Transatlantic Flight in 1919

An American, *Charles Lindbergh*, became famous for his
solo flight from New York to Paris; the Australians,
Kingsford Smith and *Bert Hinkler* made some record
flights, and *Amy Johnson*, a girl from Hull, flew alone to
Australia.

Amy Johnson

A *Spitfire* of the Second World War

Another splendid woman pilot was *Jean Batten*. The work of these men and women changed civil flying from high adventure into everyday routine, with air services to all parts of the world.

The Hawker *Hunter*

B.O.A.C. *Speedbird Comet* Jet Liner

The Second World War brought fresh developments in aircraft. Our *Hurricanes* and *Spitfires*, which beat off the German *Junkers* and *Dorniers* in the Battle of Britain in 1940, and saved this island, flew at speeds of 140 to 300 miles per hour.

By the end of the war the fastest jet aircraft were reaching speeds of about 600 miles per hour, and now, only a few years later, far greater speeds are being reached at enormous heights above the earth by jet propelled aircraft and rockets.

De Havilland *Trident*

19. THE CINEMA

For thousands of people, going to 'the pictures' is a regular weekly event, yet, like wireless and television, the cinema is a comparatively new thing in people's lives.

Photography was discovered about 1835, a Frenchman named *Daguerre* leading the way. It became popular with the Victorians, who were fond of pictures and of having their portraits painted. But paintings were expensive and only the rich could afford them. Photographs were very much cheaper, and soon many Victorian homes had photographs of all the family hanging on the walls or standing on the mantlepiece.

Charlie Chaplin and Jackie Coogan in *The Kid* (1920)

It was about sixty years later that the first moving pictures were shown on a screen. These appeared at about the same time in England, America and France, but it is now agreed that an Englishman, *Friesé-Greene,* was the inventor of the cinematograph, or 'magic box.' By 1897 'shows' were being given to the public. They were usually films of boxing matches or very short comic scenes, and were shown for a few pence in small halls and empty shops. When a train was first shown arriving at a station people rushed for the exit in panic, and a nurse had to be employed to revive the ladies who fainted!

Robbers "shooting it out" in *The Great Train Robbery*

Presently a cameraman in America had the idea of telling a story in a film, instead of just showing funny men. His company made the first real film, called *The Great Train Robbery* (1903). It was a sensational success, and people were thrilled by this new form of entertainment.

Films advanced very quickly, and within five years, the studios and producers were making films, and cinemas were being built. For once, the British were well to the front in something new, but in 1914 the war put a stop to film-making in England.

The Keystone Cops (1914) with Fatty Arbuckle on the right

America, which did not enter the war until three years later, took the lead. The Americans found that the warm, dry climate of California, with its clear air, was perfect for outdoor film-making, and in a small place called Hollywood, the film business started to grow.

Until 1927 films were silent. One could see the actors' mouths moving, but there was no sound except the music of the piano or cinema orchestra. When the story needed explanation a few sentences, called sub-titles, were flashed on the screen. Some of these silent films were among the best ever made, and the 'stars' of those days are still famous names.

Shooting a film out of doors. Wallace Beery in *Jackass Mail*

In 1927 the Americans produced the first talking picture. From this time all films were 'talkies,' and many musical films were made. Films in colour began to appear before 1939, and to-day improvements are still being made to this process.

20. WIRELESS

Telegraphy, the sending of messages along electrified wires, had been used for a great many years before the possibilities of wireless became known.

Wireless was not invented, it was discovered. Towards the end of the nineteenth century men began to experiment in sending messages without wires, using electrical impulses. A young Italian named *Marconi* came to England, and helped by Post Office engineers and a scientist named *Sir Oliver Lodge*, he took the lead in the new discoveries. Marconi's name will always be linked with the development of wireless, though it is not possible to say that any one man made a sudden, brilliant discovery.

The Testing Room at Marconi Wireless Telegraphy Works, Chelmsford, 1910

By 1898 wireless was already being used by ships to keep in touch with the shore, and the old Queen herself was able to send messages to the Prince of Wales, when he was at sea.

Wireless continued to be used in this way for a long time, and no one dreamed of its use for entertainment. During the Great War both sides found it extremely useful for sending messages in code to their forces. It was now possible to send messages to many parts of the world, but wireless telegraphy was still only used for trade and business purposes. After the war hundreds of ex-soldiers came home with considerable knowledge of wireless, and they began to build sets as a hobby.

The Marconi station at Chelmsford sent out for these enthusiasts occasional music and speech, but when the amateurs asked for permission to broadcast half an hour's music a week, the Postmaster-General refused.

He was afraid it might interfere with the telegraph services.

Broadcasting House, London

B.B.C. Savoy Hill Studio No. 1 in 1928

When the world's first broadcasting station opened in Pittsburg, America, in 1920, the Postmaster-General of Great Britain then agreed to allow a fifteen-minute programme to be broadcast once a week.

Britain continued to lag behind America until 1922, when the famous 2LO station started to broadcast from Marconi House. In the next year the British Broadcasting Company, as it was then called, had its studio at Savoy Hill, London.

In 1927, the British Broadcasting Company became the British Broadcasting Corporation. A large building was erected in 1932 for all the many departments of the B.B.C., but it soon became too small for what is now a vast organisation.

The first wireless sets were called crystal-sets, because a thin piece of quartz, or crystal, was an important part of the set. There was also a piece of wire known as the 'cat's whisker.' Since the sound was very feeble, people wore ear-phones for 'listening-in.' Tall poles were put up in many gardens because aerials had to be as high as the chimney-pots.

A Modern Studio at Broadcasting House

Improvements both in sets and programmes were soon made, and in about ten years almost every family had its wireless set, and it is now looked upon as an essential. It is curious to notice how quickly these changes take place nowadays, and how our lives can be altered in a few years.

21. TELEVISION

Lastly, television, which has now become part of our everyday lives, has developed very widely since the Second World War, but its beginnings go back to Victoria's reign.

After scientists had discovered how to send messages along electrified wires and, later, without wires, they began to wonder if they could send pictures in similar ways. This involved changing the light and shade of a picture (or image) into electric currents, sending them, receiving them and changing them back into a picture. It is a wonderful and complicated process.

Many pioneer scientists took part in the early experiments in television, but John Baird's name is the most famous. When the pioneers had discovered how to send and receive pictures or images, their next difficulty was that the very short wavelengths which are used in television were only effective for short distances. The first television aerial was set up at Alexandra Palace, on a hill in North London, near the

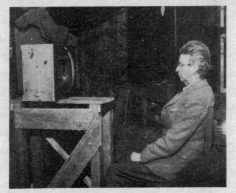

John L. Baird

A Television Studio

homes of several millions of people. The B.B.C. began sending out television programmes in 1936, but it is only since 1945 that they have had large audiences.

During the Second World War a great deal was learned about a different kind of television, called radar, and this knowledge has been used to improve television as a form of entertainment. The difficulties of distance have now been largely overcome, so that the whole of the country can enjoy the programmes. A number of commercial companies (I.T.V.), obtaining their income from advertisements, now provide television programmes, in addition to the B.B.C.

22. TOMORROW

Now that you have come to the end of this book, you may like to play a guessing game, or, better still, to start a discussion about the changes that to-morrow and the future will bring to our lives. History goes on all the time, every day, and we are part of it.

Think for a moment about the wonders which Man has achieved in the last hundred years or so: railways, motor-cars, aeroplanes, submarines, films, wireless and television, to say nothing of the discoveries of doctors and scientists. What will Man do next?

He has already walked on the Moon's surface and will one day reach the planets. Perhaps space-ships and jumbo-jets are no more wonderful than Stephenson's *Rocket* and Cugnot's steam-carriage were in their day?

But what of the problems to be overcome if air travel becomes as common as car travel to-day? Will cities have to be rebuilt, and can motor-cars survive longer than the stage-coaches did?

What about the railways? Do you think that our splendid locomotives will soon become curiosities in museums, like hansom cabs and penny-farthing bicycles?

Television has become enormously popular in a very few years. Will this mean the end of cinemas and huge crowds at football matches? Films and radio have come into our schools long since, and television lessons are already well-established.

What changes can we expect in our buildings and houses, remembering that changes come more slowly in homes than in travel? There have been plenty of new ideas since the Second World War: buildings of steel, concrete and glass, the 'prefabs,' new schools and the gay colours which are used in many new houses. It seems certain that we shall see more 'sky-scrapers' in London and our bigger cities.

Perhaps the Age of Coal and Iron is already over and we have entered a new Age of Plastics and Atomic Power, in which men will no longer labour to put brick upon brick, or to dig for fuel in coalmines. We have certainly entered an age of speed and science, in which ways of life will change more swiftly than in the past.

Will life become easy and pleasant, or dangerous, yet dull? What do you think?

ACKNOWLEDGMENTS

Grateful acknowledgment is made to the following for their permission to reproduce other drawings and photographs: The Trustees of the London Museum, pages 10 and 39; The Trustees of the National Maritime Museum, pages 30, 31, 34, 35, 106, 107, 109 and 112; The London County Council, page 40; The National Portrait Gallery, pages 45 and 157; The Trustees of the Museum of English Rural Life, Reading, page 59; Walker's Galleries Ltd., page 60; Cadbury Brothers Ltd., pages 63, 64, 148 and 149; Aerofilms Ltd., page 65; Brighton Art Gallery and Museum, page 77; Whitbread & Co. Ltd., page 80; R. E. Trevithick, page 90; 19th Century Prints, pages 90 and 92; London Transport, page 99; The Trustees of the Tate Gallery, page 103; The Times, page 121; The Council of Industrial Design, pages 122-124, 140 and 142; The National Coal Board, pages 127 and 128; The National Buildings Record, page 138; The Trustees of the Victoria & Albert Museum, page 142; The British Gas Council, page 140; The Cunard Steamship Co. Ltd., pages 113-114; The Trustees of the Imperial War Museum, pages 115, 116, 167, 176 and 177; Picture Post Library, pages 117, 168 and 185; The Proprietors of Punch, page 153; The Ford Motor Co. Ltd., pages 164 and 166; The Autocar, page 165; The Central Office of Information, page 166; Topical Press, page 172; Keystone Press Agency Ltd., pages 174, 175 and 178-179; Vickers Ltd., page 178; The Hawker Siddeley Group, page 179; British Overseas Airways Corporation, page 180; The United States Information Service, pages 181 and 184; Metro Goldwyn Mayer, page 183; The British Broadcasting Corporation, pages 186-188; Fox Photos Ltd., page 189; Crown Copyright: From an exhibit in the Science Museum, South Kensington, pages 92, 96, 101, 109, 162, 163 and 165; Crown Copyright: From a drawing in the Science Museum, South Kensington, page 93; By courtesy of the Director of the Science Museum, South Kensington, pages 174-175 and 178.

Acknowledgment is also made for the use of drawings on pages 46 and 47 by E. J. Warne, from John Gloag's English Furniture, and for the photograph on page 42 by John Gloag; pages 50-53, 143-146 and 151-152 from Iris Brooke's English Costume of the 18th Century and English Costume of the 19th Century; pages 54, 154 and 155 from Iris Brooke's English Children's Costume Since 1775; pages 24 to 27 and 104 by T. L. Poulton, from The Story of the Wheel by G. M. Boumphrey. Originals of the china reproduced on pages 48-49 are in the Victoria and Albert Museum.